The Four and the One

In Praise of String Quartets

To my friends in music.

The Lafayette Quartet

From left, Ann Elliott-Goldschmid, first violin; Joanna Hood, viola; Pamela Highbaugh, cello; Sharon Stanis, second violin.

The Four and the One

In Praise of String Quartets

by David Rounds
with the help of
the Lafayette Quartet

Lost
Coast Press
Fort Bragg, California

The Four and the One: In Praise of String Quartets
Copyright © 1999 by David Rounds

For information phone (707) 964-9520.
For VISA and MasterCard orders, please call (800) 773-7782.
Write to Lost Coast Press, 155 Cypress Street, Fort Bragg CA 95437
or visit www.cypresshouse.com

Library of Congress Catalog Card No. 98-067097

ISBN No. 1-882897-26-9

Cover illustration: Braque, Georges,
Musical Forms with the Words "Fete" and "journ"
(1913) 36¼" x 23½", oil, pencil, and charcoal on canvas
Philadelphia Museum of Art:
The Louise and Walter Arensberg Collection

Cover design by Gopa Design

By the same author
Coalitions (a novel); *Celebrisi's Journey* (a novel); *Cannonball River
Tales* (children's stories); *Perfecting a Piece of the World: Arthur
Imperatore and the Blue Collar Aristocrats of A-P-A* (non-fiction)

Book production by Cypress House, Fort Bragg, CA 95437

Printed in Canada

2 4 6 8 9 7 5 3 1

First Edition

The Four and the One

In Praise of String Quartets

Mercutio, thou consort'st with Romeo.
—William Shakespeare

Table of Contents

Appendix A

A Listener's Guide to the Quartet Repertory

Appendix B

Two Appreciations

Prelude

An Addiction to Quartets

On a Sunday afternoon in March, outside a Methodist church in Mill Valley, California, four musicians from Canada stand in the sunlight. They're wearing long black formal dresses, as if to identify themselves as leaders of a ceremony. Two of the musicians are holding their violins, and one her viola, at chest level, in the manner of string players at rest: right hand free, while the three outer fingers of the left hand curl around the neck of the instrument, so that it dangles to the waist. The thumb and forefinger hold the bow, letting it descend at an angle. As for the cellist, she has left her instrument in the vestry, and as I walk past, she is busy shaping with her hands something she is describing to the others, who are laughing. After a pause, the four women suddenly nod to each other, as if cueing the start of a musical phrase, then turn and walk inside.

Around the corner of the building, a mix of Marin County, in three generations, is streaming through the glass front doors. It's a local crowd; clearly many people know each other. Probably no more than half a dozen people in the audience have driven, as I have, more than twenty minutes for this concert. The earliest arrivals are the retired couples, dressed in the same sports coats and pastel dresses they wore, perhaps, to this morning's church service. Then the mainstay of classical music audiences, the over-forty professionals: teachers and government

1

workers, bearded stockbrokers in turtlenecks, corporate lawyers with many-tiered earrings brushing the padded shoulders of their silk blouses. There's a scattering of younger couples with children, and lastly a few teenagers who have arrived with their parents; spotting one another, they stand in pairs and trios in the vestibule, their hips cocked and their weight on one foot while they glance around shyly at this ritual of their elders. Gradually the participants file into the sanctuary, past a wiry matron dispensing programs at the door. On the dais before the altar, the furniture of religion, pulpit and lectern, have been displaced by the furniture of music: four straight-backed chairs facing four music stands. The concert audience sidles into the semicircular rows of pews.

The low C of a cello rasps faintly from the vestry. Before the first note of their performance, the string players are already exercising one of their subtlest skills: matching pitches on those cranky Renaissance artifacts they make their music on. Soon the musicians stride on stage, smiling. They bow — an archaism which, in Western countries, only performing artists are called upon to make — and the audience replies with another ceremonial gesture, the striking together of their palms. Then the four women of the Lafayette Quartet sit down, arrange the folds of their skirts, plant their feet, raise their bows, bind themselves together in an intense mutual glance, nod suddenly, and begin.

Now one of the most magical of human discoveries fills the hall — the sound of the bowed string. It's a sound I've been pledged to since, at an early age, I gave away my heart to music. Josef Haydn is the first composer on the Lafayette's program today, but in my childhood, Bach was my first idol, and his music for stringed instruments my first addiction. In the mid-1940's, before I reached the age of five, I scratched many a 78 on the family victrola as I listened to the Brandenburg Concertos. But it was not until I was a teenager that I heard my first quartets. My late father, Stowell Rounds, had helped found a series of chamber music concerts in our Connecticut town, just as many other music lovers were doing elsewhere for the growing population of postwar suburban audiences. His series, called the Candlelight Concerts, first featured local musicians, then gradu-

2

ally drew professionals from nearby New York. Among them was the already famous Juilliard String Quartet.

From my special spot in the side balcony of the old Wilton Congregational Church, I could gaze down, as I remember, directly upon the four men of the Juilliard as they were seated in a semi-circle on the dais. The violist, Rafael Hillyer, played almost immediately below me. Black-browed, elegant, and impassive, he — and I — could look across the dais to the first violinist, Robert Mann, as he scribbled passionately on his strings with his bow like a mad writer possessed. Between them sat Isidore Cohen, the second violinist, round-faced and bald, laboring solemnly in the trenches of an inner part, and silver-haired Claus Adam, the cellist, serene and regal as he held up the edifice of music with the foundation of the bass line.[1]

Great performances of classical music, we are taught in our star-dazzled culture, are the responsibility of individuals. We take conductors, opera divas, and instrumental soloists as our musical heroes. But, as I watched the apparently ill-matched members of the Juilliard, I understood that quartets were different. Clearly these four men's musicianship qualified them to take turns on great stages as soloists; yet they chose not to. Instead they made their music in churches and small halls, playing as a foursome. What they offered was not an image of heroism, but a demonstration of community. Their tossing their melodies and harmonies back and forth across the church dais was much like the ball-handling of the scruffy infielders who, on other Sundays, I yelled at from the balcony at Yankee Stadium. Watching and listening, I knew that the greatest music, like the greatest of games, is not after all played by individual stars, but by teams. And I was hooked.

Performing quartets often begin their concerts, as the Lafayette has done today in Mill Valley, with the music of Haydn. The choice is appropriate. It was Haydn who founded the quartet tradition. In the 1760's, he was one of several composers who began writing dance-like suites for two violins, a viola, and a cello. For such a combination of instruments, it makes sense to highlight one of the two violins. On its higher strings, the violin has greater carrying power than almost any other instrument,

3

and for a string quartet, a composer's obvious choice is to assign all the melodies to the first violin, so that the audience can hear the tunes. The other instruments can fill in the accompaniment. But Haydn had a different idea. Because the sounds made by the quartet's four instruments are so similar, he thought it might be possible to make their voices equal. The first violin would not be the star soloist; it would be a member of a team.

In the Haydn quartet that the Lafayette is performing today, the instruments seem to be conversing. As the tunes and tune-fragments pass around the players' semi-circle, the listener hears questions and answers, pleas and consents, assertions and counter-arguments, debates and resolutions. In Haydn's hands, and in the hands of composers who followed him, the quartet became a musical paradigm of human interaction on a small scale. The orchestra, by contrast, recapitulates in music an entire society, while the soloist recounts the drama of the individual heart. Halfway between them, the four equal voices of a quartet, and the four quartet-players performing together as equals, bespeak the life of the family and the community of friends. Each member is playing a part that takes its chief meaning from its role in the group. The instruments and the players are four, but the music is one.

The quartet's power to imitate human interaction is made greater by the close resemblance between the sound of bowed stringed instruments and the sound of the human voice. The violin sometimes so closely resembles a woman's voice that if a soprano is singing on an open vowel in a duet with a violin, a listener may have to strain to tell them apart.[2] Further, two violins, a viola, and a cello have almost the same range as a vocal quartet — soprano, alto, tenor, and bass — and the instruments can reduplicate almost any spoken inflection. Therefore, they can imitate, with great subtlety, the vocal expression of almost any emotion. Thus the quartet can convey personal feelings precisely as we most often experience them in real life — in response to, and in the company of, other people.

All this has made the quartet form irresistible to composers. Mozart and Beethoven succeeded Haydn as masters of the form, and since their time, most composers in the Western classical tradition have written some of their most intense, most ambitious, most personal, and most beautiful music for string quartet. Today, even more than in the past, almost every writer of classical music attempts to prove himself or herself worthy of the word "composer" by writing at least one work for two violins, a viola, and a cello.

Nor does the quartet survive merely as a medium of European classical styles. Composers from Africa and Asia have adapted the quartet to their own musics, as have pop and jazz musicians, including Jimi Hendrix, Elvis Costello, John Zorn, and the Beatles. Some classical forms seem in danger of crashing like threatened species, but the gregarious adaptability of quartets has made them resistant to obsolescence. When I see an ad for the Turtle Island String Quartet playing a gig of strings jazz in a Berkeley coffee house, and when my niece studying in Namibia sends me a tape of the Soweto String Quartet playing South African pop, then I can hope that I will never have to do without my fix of quartet music.

Because so many masterpieces have been written for quartet, and because of its ability to take on the color of new musical styles, quartets remain more compelling to performers, and more popular among audiences, than many other kinds of classical music. In the United States and Canada, over 1,400 organizations present concerts of chamber music, of which string quartets are by far the most dominant form. Most of these organizations, moreover, were established during the past twenty years. There is more interest now in quartets than there has been at any time since they were invented about 235 years ago. Thirty years ago, there were about 30 professional string quartet ensembles based in North America; now, there are nearly 200.[3]

Still, I always look around at quartet concerts to see if the house is full, as it is today for the Lafayette's performance in Mill Valley. Like many classical music lovers, I worry that audiences may be aging and that funding is contracting. Since the late 1970's, there has actually been a bull market in quartets, and in other forms of classical music performance as well, but it is a market that has peaked and has perhaps already entered a long decline. The classical audiences of the future are not being created, because music instruction has been removed from so many public schools.[4] Symphony orchestras run at increasingly burdensome deficits, and some face bankruptcy.[5] In the United States, small musical organizations like quartets and presenters of quartet concerts will perhaps be hurt most by the gutting of the National Endowment for the Arts.[6] No doubt there will always be symphonies and quartets, but it is by no means certain that it will always be so easy to hear them.

This book in praise of string quartets is written partly, then, in a spirit of combativeness. The arts are under attack, especially in the United States, and it behooves us who are devoted to the arts to remind ourselves, and others, of what the arts are for and what artists must do to bring them to us. Nowadays, whatever role we play in the arts we must play aggressively. As for myself, I can't defend my own favorite art of quartets by playing them, or writing them, but my part in the music is nevertheless an essential one. I am a listener. And on behalf of other listeners, both those who love quartets and those who might come to love them, I want to be a herald for the greatness of this precious and vulnerable art.

The other motive for this book is fulfillment of a youthful vow. When I was a boy, I wanted to be a musician, but my slow fingers at the piano discouraged me. I resolved to be a writer instead. After college, I returned home to Connecticut to write my first novel, a political love story about two interracial couples — a white man and his black wife, and her brother and a white woman who falls in love with him. Every morning, before beginning to write, I would listen to music for courage and inspiration. As the months passed and the chapters accumulated, all the records on the phonograph became string quartets, and then the quartets winnowed themselves down to one. It was the Juilliard's recording of the fourteenth quartet of Beethoven, his Opus 131, in C sharp minor.[7]

I knew of the consensus among musicians that this work, which was completed in 1826, was still the greatest of all quartets. As I listened again and again, I heard in the music what I wanted to say with my novel about gender and race. The four instruments were speaking of the wisdom of affirmation that

6

can be found on the other side of suffering, and of the joy of forgiveness reached through love. Like the quartet, too, my novel intertwined the voices and thoughts of four people. Looking back on that year, I can see now that, without realizing it, I was attempting my own string quartet in the best way I knew how — with words.

In subsequent years, when this first novel, and then my second novel, had been published and forgotten, I gradually became clearer about my own limitations. I write non-fiction now. But I resolved that, even if I couldn't rival the splendor of quartets in my own stories, I would still attempt a book that would measure the power that quartets exert over me. What is this magic that compels devotion from so many people? Why does this communal, old-fashioned art — created at the outset of the industrial revolution, and written for instruments built with seventeenth-century technology — still thrive amid the hostile environment of modern mass society?

It is fitting that we use the phrase "string quartet" to describe not only the written music, but the team of performers. For a technical analysis of a piece of music, one only needs the written page, but to give an account of the music as it is experienced by listeners, one cannot leave out the players. How a piece is performed depends on the performers, and no performance is the same as any other. This is especially true of quartets. Quartet music is extremely difficult to play well, and in the pursuit of excellence, professional performers work together for years, often for decades. Their association can become so intense that many players describe it as a kind of marriage. Inevitably, the professional and personal relations of the four players pour out into the harmony and battle of the four voices in the music. The emotional electricity characteristic of quartet performances, then, flows as much from the responses of the players to each other as from the interweaving currents of notes written on the composer's page. From our seats in the audience, we are not just listening to music. We are witnessing a four-part communion whose medium is sound.

This is my book about quartets, then — about both kinds, the music and the players. The focus is on the engagement of four people with music. The story eavesdrops on one string quartet, the Lafayette Quartet, in rehearsal of one string quartet, Alexander Borodin's Quartet No. 2. The four women of the Lafayette are observed as a working community which is still in good health after twelve years of grueling tours, endless rehearsals, financial hardship, and unavoidable interpersonal clashes. To set the Lafayette's work in context, the book offers histories of quartet writing and also of quartet performance, but technical discussion is kept to a minimum. In following the Lafayette's career, the book examines the problematic career of quartet musicians in general, who must endure the consequences of a paradox. As performers of quartets they enjoy prestige and admiration, but it is almost impossible for them to make a living from performing the music. Finally, as an appendix, I have added a listeners' guide to the quartet repertory, together with appreciations of two string quartets — in the hope that, having read of my love affair with quartets, readers will want to pursue their own.

I have chosen, deliberately, lesser known quartets as my subject. Borodin's Quartet No. 2 is elegant, beautiful, inviting, and already familiar to many listeners, but it is not a great star in the quartet literature. The Lafayette, for its part, is recognized among musicians and quartet enthusiasts on both sides of the Atlantic as one of the excellent younger quartets, with a warm string sound, a talent for distinctive interpretations, and a flair for Eastern European music. However, like the Borodin, the members of the Lafayette are not stars, and although their career is by now secure, they perhaps will never know much fame. Most quartets don't. Their music is not written for stars, but for teams.

Classical music audiences are by no means immune to the appeal of celebrity, and they are happy to fill a hall to gawk at the face that belongs to a famous name. But quartet audiences are an exception. I may well have been the only person at the Lafayette's concert in Mill Valley, except the concert organizers, who had heard of this Canadian quartet before. The hall was filled anyway. The listeners around me had come not for stars, but for music. They recognized, though they might not have expressed it as I do, that the art of quartets cuts through the fantasy of celebrity and wealth that dominates our cultural life and reveals, instead, the realities of human interaction. Of course, it is true that, despite the limitations of their medium, a handful of performing quartets in fact have managed to become famous. But this book is not about stardom. It is about an art that is communal and about artists whose power is drawn from working together.

To help me tell this story, the members of the Lafayette Quartet — Ann Elliott-Goldschmid, Sharon Stanis, Joanna Hood, and Pamela Highbaugh — submitted to many hours of interviews and intrusions on their rehearsals over five weeks during the course of the 1993-94 concert season. I owe them a great debt for their generosity, their frankness, and their superb musical integrity. I am grateful, too, to all the other musicians — quartet players, composers, recording engineers, concert presenters, artists' managers, and listeners — whom I interviewed for this book. Any errors of fact or interpretation are my own.

I. The Quartet as Music

1. Historical: A Consort of Violins

Chamber Music

By a generally accepted, somewhat flexible definition, chamber music requires three conditions. First, two or more players or singers are making music together. Second, each of the participants is assigned his or her own part, so that no part is doubled. Third, the music proceeds without the guidance of a conductor. String quartets, then, are a form of chamber music. The first violin, second violin, viola, and cello are each playing a separate musical line, so that there are four instrumental voices sounding at once.

In the strings section of a symphony orchestra, too, four parts can usually be heard: the notes for first violin, for second violin, for viola, and finally for cello and double bass, which very often play the same line, the bass an octave below the cello. But these four musical lines are the work of many players: there may be twelve first violinists on stage, ten second violinists, eight violists, six cellists, and four bassists — a total of forty. Similarly, a vocal quartet and a 100-voice chorus can both sing four-part harmony. In this sense, then, what distinguishes chamber music is not the number of parts, but the number of voices. The differences lie not so much in musical complexity as in the volume and the quality of the sound.

By 1550, what we now think of as vocal chamber music was being performed by amateur singers in their own homes. It was music expressly written to be performed, and also to be heard, by small groups of people, in relatively small indoor spaces — in chambers. The performance space matched the volume of sound. Later, in the eighteenth century, Haydn and his contemporaries wrote string quartets for performance in small halls in aristocrats' palaces. In our century, unfortunately, chamber musicians often perform in large halls built for symphony orchestras, so that larger audiences can be accommodated. But the bigger the hall, the more faintly the music is heard. Four players cannot make the sound of forty. Further, the aural and visual drama of the interaction of the four performers is dissipated by the distance between the stage and the far-flung audience. String quartets are best heard and seen in the small spaces they were written for.

Once a chamber ensemble reaches a certain size — of more than, usually, eight members — the musical teamwork becomes unwieldy. There are so many minds at work that decisions must be left to a musician whose chief or only task is to lead: namely, a conductor. Inevitably, orchestral and choral musicians submerge all their constituent voices into a massed sound, and the players sacrifice their independence to a leader, for the sake of group power. The audience, for its part, is no longer witnessing a community of equals, but a single forceful personality mastering a crowd. At the other extreme in the social spectrum of music is the soloist, who is both lead player and lead decision-maker. The soloist may be performing alone, or else to the accompaniment of one or many instruments; what distinguishes solo music is not solitude but focus on a single sensibility and an individual voice. Standing between the two extremes, chamber music draws strength from both. It preserves the separate voices while embedding them with each other. The players are a cooperative society made up of individuals who remain distinct.

This three-step progression from soloist to team music to the music of the mass is neither a modern invention nor a Western one. It exists in all musics. The lone harpist or pipe-player — the small group of specialists on strings, flutes, and drums — the village chorus of voices, drums, or horns — all are ancient forms. To define chamber music as the string quartet, the piano

11

trio, and the wind and brass quintets, with their variations, is to listen much too exclusively. African choirs of tuned drums also make chamber music. So do the various groupings of instruments — voice, drums, melodic strings, drone strings, and flute — in the musics of North and South India. The artistic power of these chamber forms is equal to our own. In our tradition, members of jazz groups, barbershop quartets, madrigal groups, and rock bands are all by definition chamber players.

Before the Quartet

In Europe, the peasant dance band and the monastic choir were the medieval antecedents of modern chamber music. For the string quartet in particular, secular dance music provided the technology. The early forms of bowed stringed instruments acted as lead players in village dance bands. The modern violin family itself — violin, viola, and cello — was founded in the mid-sixteenth century, and the new instruments distinguished themselves by their unprecedented loudness, and by their uncanny ability to imitate the human voice. The violin, especially, could project a melody over the heads of other instruments, including percussion, even outdoors, in the midst of a noisy dance. It gradually replaced the older rebecs, fiddles, and viols as band leader, and it still leads in Gypsy music, mariachi music, klezmer music and other folk forms. The violin was so closely associated with uninhibited rustic footwork, in fact, that the Vatican declared it unfit to be heard in churches. The violin ban, never successfully enforced, was not lifted until 1749.

While dance music provided the physical tools, sacred vocal music created the intellectual basis for the future development of string quartets. Monastic choirs discovered polyphony, which arises when voices sing two or more melodies together at the same time. In its earliest stages in church music, in the tenth century, monks sang more or less the same Gregorian chant melodies moving together at two pitches, in parallel fourths and fifths — probably to accommodate the natural difference between the bass and the tenor voice. This first polyphony was called organum. The story of church music for the next 500 years is the elaboration of this idea.

As the monastic musicians chanted organum, they succumbed to the temptation to vary what one of the voices was singing. They gradually realized that entirely different melodies could be sung at the same time; or — even more interesting — the same melody could be sung from different starting points, so that it would overlap itself in imitation. This was the canon. When musicians began singing against each other in these ways, they found some of the resulting intervals and chords to be more pleasing than others. In order to achieve a more satisfying concerted sound, they learned to vary the melodies to manipulate the intervals. The eventual result of these experiments was the discovery of harmony and key relations, which since the early Renaissance have been the hallmark of Western music.

Anyone who has sung a round is familiar with polyphony's magical trick. In a round, which is the strictest form of canon, a melody is begun in one voice only. It is then continued in that voice while, at the same time, another voice takes it up from the beginning. A third voice begins the melody while the others continue, then perhaps a fourth voice enters, and even a fifth. The result is that the melody is heard sounding against itself at different intervals. Everyone is singing the melody, but the totality of the sound is a series of constantly shifting chords. As for the singers, they are doing two things at once: they are singing their own part, and they are creating harmony. They are distinct individuals engaged in a joint creation. This is chamber music.

Polyphony spread first to secular vocal music, with the madrigal and its many forbears and relatives, and then to instrumental music, with its strings, winds, and keyboards. By the middle of the sixteenth century, amateur musicians among the aristocracy and the middle classes were playing and singing polyphonic music. Among the most popular were two forms: settings of love poems for voices — what we now think of as the madrigal tradition — and music without words for consorts of viols. At the time, the soft-voiced viols, not the violins, were the instruments for playing genteel string music indoors. These instruments' sloping shoulders and thick-set bodies easily distinguish them from the slimmer, more round-shouldered violins. They are now largely obsolete, except for the bass viol, which is the modern double-bass.

With both the madrigal group and the viol consort, the artistic and social foundations of the string quartet had already been built. The social equality among players was matched by a musical equality among the parts. The purest polyphony, the round, attains perfect musical egalitarianism, since everyone sings exactly the same thing. In general, no musical type suits a musical family or a group of musical friends better than the various Renaissance polyphonic chamber forms. Everyone has a chance to sing the melody, and everyone makes an equal contribution to the musical whole. This is the reason that the Renaissance madrigal continues to grow in popularity among amateur singers even now, half a millennium after its invention.

In the late Renaissance, there was still no need for the string quartet, even well after the violin family had been established. The gentle voices of the consort of viols were already ideal for polyphony. When all the parts are playing much the same melody, the idiosyncratic character of each individual part is secondary. The louder, more vibrant, more soloistic voices of the violin family promote personal assertion, which is not appropriate for polyphony. The voices of the violin and cello, especially, are pushy; they don't know their place. But to the Renaissance ear, music spoke of social harmony.

> For government, though high and low and lower,
> Put into parts, doth keep in one consent,
> Congreeing in a full and natural close,
> Like music.

Thus the Duke of Exeter in *Henry V.* [8] In Shakespeare's simile, the different pitch-ranges of the musical instruments in polyphony represent the different levels of society — "high, low, and lower." It is precisely because the voices stay in their own range to sing the common tune that they can create the harmony. At the time, the word "division" was a popular word for polyphonic music. Division did not create divisiveness, but agree-

14

ment. As the Duke says, what is "put into parts doth keep in one consent."

The Invention of the Quartet

Between 1650 and 1750, the preference for polyphony gradually faded before a fascination with the solo voice. The madrigalist was replaced in popularity by the opera singer, and the consort of viols by the solo violin. This was the first great age of the violin concerto. Many of the leading composers — Corelli, Locatelli, Vivaldi and Tartini among them — were violin virtuosos who toured their own pieces and established once and for all their instrument's unrivaled power to sing. In sympathy with the age, chamber music shifted from the polyphonic group to the soloistic singing of a lead melodist. The consort of viols gave way to forms that showcased the first violin, backed by a light-textured accompaniment.

The most significant of the new chamber music forms was the trio sonata. Despite its name, this ensemble consisted of four instruments, not three: first and second violin, cello, and harpsichord or other keyboard. The cello duplicated the bass line on the keyboard instead of contributing a separate part; therefore the sonata was a "trio," because the cello and keyboard counted as one. In the trio sonata, then, the cello was downgraded and the viola was absent. Musical interest centered on florid melodies played by the first violin. These fanciful melodic elaborations, in the new *style galant*, were the aural counterpart of the torrid visual extravagances of Rococo art and architecture. As a popular chamber form requiring four players, the trio sonata belongs among the precursors of the string quartet. But in its display of the first violin as a solo singer, it was closer to the violin concerto and the sonata for violin and keyboard.

The string quartet descends equally from lower-born origins. Like modern teenagers with their territorial boomboxes, eighteenth-century adults liked to listen to music outdoors. Small ensembles of musicians would play easy-listening chamber music — variously called divertimenti, serenades, and cassations — in the streets, perhaps beneath their girlfriends' windows. A harpsichord, standard in the trio sonata and other sophisticated forms, could hardly be wheeled down the street. This may be the reason that, when the music called for strings alone, the viola was brought back to fill in the middle of the harmony. When Josef Haydn, probably just before 1760, began composing pieces for two violins, viola, and cello — what are now recognized as his first string quartets — he called them divertimenti and wrote them in outdoor-music form, with five dance-like movements. His first ten quartets presented the first violin as a *style-galant* soloist, with the second violin, viola, and cello as a backup string band.[9]

The written records of the time do not reveal whether Haydn's first string quartets were the first to be written by anyone. Other composers around 1760 were also writing serenades for two violins, viola, and cello. What is certain is that Haydn was the innovator who understood the extraordinary possibilities of the form that had come his way. He had in his hands a band of four strong voices, very similar in sound, each of them capable of singing out as a soloist. Why then assign all the interesting music to the first violin, while distributing among the others the leavings of simple accompaniment, as in a trio sonata?

Here was a chance to reinvent chamber music, to revive the old musical friendships of Renaissance polyphony. But the restrained viols, whose gentle music represented dutiful subservience to the social order, were not the right instruments for an age that was already fascinated by the drama of the individual and that was testing new limits to the rights of man. What was needed was a consort of violins. It would speak for a civilization that valued the personal voice, but that also feared revolution and anarchy. It would represent in sound the correct balance between the one and the many.

Nothing was more important to the creation of this new art form than Haydn's revival of the viola. Originally, before 1600, the instrument had developed in two forms — a smaller alto, with a body of about sixteen inches, two inches longer than the violin, and then a tenor, which was as much as two and half inches longer than the alto. But by 1700, the alto voice in orchestral strings sections had been usurped by the more resonant second violin, and the viola was reduced to a tenor part that often merely doubled the cello an octave higher. In chamber music during this period, the viola was needed hardly at all. Very few violas were made in the first decades of the 1700's, presumably because there were enough left over from the previous century. Viola parts in orchestras were handed to the least competent players, with the result that violists and their instrument sank to a status of low esteem that has not been shaken off entirely even 250 years later.[10]

The viola is the least aggressive voice of the violin family. Its tone is covered and darkened. The restraint in its voice results from its size. What we hear from a stringed instrument is not the vibrations of the strings; they are too small to create much agitation in the air around them. Rather, the vibrations of the strings are transferred through the bridge and the soundpost to the top plate and backplate of the instrument's wooden body and to the air within the body. These masses are large enough to push the air surrounding them with considerable force. The resulting vibrations travel through the air to our eardrums, which vibrate in turn. In a well built violin and cello, the wood and the air cavity vibrate in sympathy with the open strings. But, in the viola, the body of the instrument is not large enough to resonate properly with its two lowest strings. A perfectly resonating viola would be the size of a guitar and would have to be bowed between the knees. Since the instrument is acoustically too small, its sound is muted. Even on some of the best instruments, the lower strings can sound nasal and querulous.

In these disadvantages, Haydn heard advantages. To his ears, the viola's dark and subtle voice, by its contrast with the brightness of the violins and with the depth and vibrancy of the cello, added richness and density to string writing. For his symphonies, he discarded the common practice of writing perfunctory viola parts, and he recruited violists for the orchestra at Esterháza, where he was court conductor and composer for thirty years. In chamber music, he saw that it was the viola that would create the characteristic string quartet sound. With it, the quartet reached a depth of aural perspective that opened vistas beyond the elegant tapestry of the trio sonata's *style galant.*

When the viola is given the melody, its special voice expands the quartet's emotional range. Its huskiness can quickly establish a somber mood, and its querulousness is perfect for making a sarcastic comment. Haydn considered the viola so central to the quartet that he preferred to play the instrument himself when he took part in quartet performances. Numerous others among the great quartet composers have made the same choice, including Mozart (who was a virtuoso on the instrument), Beethoven (who is said to have played stringed instruments badly), and Schubert, Mendelssohn, Dvořák, Britten, and Hindemith.[11]

Between 1769 and 1772, Haydn added eighteen new quartets to his first ten. In them he wrestled at closer and closer quarters with the contradictions inherent in a harmonious consort of four soloistic voices. Despite an amazingly prolific inventiveness, he did not discover easily a new middle ground between the soloistic *style galant* and the old egalitarian polyphony. It was not obvious how to overcome the melodic dominance of the first violin, especially in songful slow movements, unless it were to revert to the older style. In fact, in his fifth set of quartets, published as Opus 20 and written in 1772, Haydn sometimes returned to polyphony, most notably in the use of fugues. Mozart, meanwhile, a teenager at the time, had already written ten quartets, and after hearing Haydn's Opus 20 he immediately wrote six more that also made use of the polyphonic style.

But the older style could not represent the spirit of Haydn's times. The Age of Enlightenment esteemed above all the fine art of civilized human relations. The skills of that art were developed in the practice of conversation. Talk was meant to sparkle with a refined expression of wit and sentiment, of gaiety and elegance, of reasonableness and naturalness. In successful conversation, people don't parrot each other with imitated phrases, as if they were speaking in polyphony. Nor do they enjoy confining themselves to an accompaniment of Mm-hms, while a single bore, aspiring to be a soloist, interminably holds forth about his own private concerns. Instead, people in conversation remark and comment, listen and reply, question and answer, dispute points of view and, perhaps, harmoniously agree at the end. Refined conversation among social equals — among men and women like those who populate Jane Austen's novels — this was the Enlightenment ideal that Haydn sought to embody in quartet music.

In 1781, eight years after writing his Opus 20, Haydn produced another set of six quartets, his Opus 33, and he called them "quartets" for the first time. In promotional letters urging patrons to buy copies, he announced that the music had been "written in a new and special way." The first violin continues its dominance in these pieces. But the composer granted the second violin, viola, and cello far more power to answer back than he had given them before, and their replies were not mere parrotings, as in polyphony, but amendments and rebuttals. The composer also allowed the lower voices occasionally to initiate the conversation; the viola and cello in duet state the melody first, for example, in the slow movement of the second quartet of the set. Haydn had set as his goal an equality among the voices, and even today this remains the ideal sought by for composers of string quartets.[12]

In this new music of conversation between equals, Haydn found perfect employment for the style of melodic variation which came to be known as the sonata form. Developed since the 1750's by numerous composers, including Haydn, the sonata form preserved the polyphonic style by revolutionizing it. The sonata rejects the confinements of strict imitation. Instead, it modifies and develops melodies, chops them up and plays them in new keys, recasts them and returns to them, and alternates them in contrast with other melodies of different moods. A small change in melody or harmony can express dispute or concord, while an extended variation may suggest an inspired commentary by one speaker upon another's idea. Above all, in Haydn's music, a sudden stop in the flow, an entry from an unexpected quarter, or a slyly modified imitation reduplicates the thrusts of aristocratic verbal wit.

These musical conversations became quickly popular among amateur players, who took to quartets just as, two cen-

turies earlier, they had taken to the polyphonic chamber music
for singers and for viols. Thus was established the tradition of
amateur string quartet playing which has continued unbroken
to this day.[13] In Haydn's time, thousands of string quartets were
written to serve the amateur market, especially in the Austrian
empire and in the German and Italian states. Composers would
advertise their quartets "on subscription" — that is, for sale in
advance of publication. Of the many quartet composers of the
late eighteenth century, though, only Haydn and Mozart are still
remembered today in frequent quartet performances.

In 1782, upon hearing Haydn's Opus 33 quartets, Mozart,
now a mature composer of 26, himself returned to the string
quartet form. He began composing a set of six quartets which
he dedicated to Haydn in acknowledgment of his elder
contemporary's discovery of the new way. (Musicians now call
these six pieces the Mozart "Haydn" quartets.) With the composition of twelve of his twenty operas already behind him,
Mozart could apply Haydn's techniques to his own genius for
expressing character in vocal music. In some parts of the Mozart
quartets, the four string players seem to be a quartet of opera
singers standing downstage at the end of the act, each confessing his or her private conflict or else all four joining in a shared
triumph. Operatic passages of dissonance that seem to be expressing pain resolve into sequences of light-hearted playful-
ness that draw on the spirit of outdoor music. As in so much of
Mozart's music, a dark thread is woven into a bright fabric, often so intimately that the listener can hardly tell if the music is
expressive of sadness or delight. In this way Mozart anticipates
the Romantic century.

Beethoven

The Age of Enlightenment perished with the French Revolution and the Napoleonic wars. It was Beethoven who discovered how the string quartet, which had served the ideals of the
Enlightenment, could be modified to express the new sensibilities of the Romantic era. But he made his debut in quartet composition cautiously and hesitantly. He published the six pieces

of Opus 18 in 1801, when he was already over thirty and well established in Vienna as a composer. The Opus 18 quartets were for the most part conservative: they recall the wit and sentiment of Haydn much more than the impassioned drama of Mozart. Only brief passages prefigure the transformation that Beethoven was already working upon music through his piano sonatas.

Four years later, in 1805 and 1806, when he was more sure of his new Romantic style, Beethoven published the three revolutionary quartets of Opus 59, which are often called the Razumovsky quartets, after the Russian count who was their dedicatee. In these pieces, the aristocratic salon has vanished. Not merely short introductions, as in Opus 18, but whole movements now call up the pre-verbal shouts and sobs of unedited emotion. In Beethoven's new way, Haydn's witty surprises became jagged, painful contrasts. Mozart's operatic dissonances were now so prevalent and pronounced that the more conservative of performers and audiences declared the new quartets unplayable and unlistenable. But others recognized in them the future of European music.

By shifting the quartet's emotional content, Beethoven shifted its social setting. Listening to his quartets, we are no longer sitting in on a conversation among friends. We are following instead the ebb and flow of feelings within an individual heart. Beethoven's solitude as a deaf and eccentric bachelor, and his belief as a Romantic artist in the primacy of personal concerns, had turned the quartet inwards. The composer's contemporaries heard this change of direction as clearly as we do now —although they did not always like it. According to Beethoven's friend and amanuensis, Anton Schindler, the composer "wanted the quartets to be performed in the same manner as the sonatas, for they paint states of mind, as do the majority of the sonatas."[14]

Beethoven's last five quartets, the so-called "late quartets," written between 1822 and 1826, only deepen the inwardness.[15] The four strings seem to be speaking a conversation of thoughts. Generations of audiences have had the sense of stepping through the walls of a deaf man's silence to listen in on the inner voices of a mind as it came to terms with isolation and death. It was the third of these, Opus 131, that I played every morning on the phonograph during that spring, thirty years ago, when I was writing my first novel. I was experimenting with recording my four characters' thoughts. I placed mental voices together in dialogue as they thought about each other. What other music could I have listened to as I wrote?

By adapting the quartet to the concerns of Romanticism, Beethoven showed composers who followed him that, by extension, the quartet could also be adapted to other sensibilities that might emerge from the forward motion of history. Since Beethoven's time, composers have used the voices of the quartet to imitate the communing of lovers, as in Alexander Borodin's Quartet No. 2; to represent the combined voices and characters of a people, as in Antonín Dvořák's quartets, which are woven of folksongs; to record the struggle of a cowed population against a ruthless state, as in Dmitri Shostakovich's anti-Soviet quartet-tragedies; to portray the purity of nature, as in the quartets of the post-modern Canadian composer R. Murray Schafer.

The Quartet in the Nineteenth Century

The great Austrian and German composers who were born during Beethoven's lifetime — Franz Schubert, Felix Mendelssohn, and Robert Schumann — all wrote string quartets. But after 1848, the quartet was eclipsed by other forms. Instead of chamber music, the new age of industrialism and nationalism favored two other paradigms — the soloist as individual and the symphony as mass. The contemporary imagination was captured by the quasi-military hundred-piece orchestra commanded by fierce Teutonic dictators wielding their swagger-stick batons — or, to adopt a related, equally paradigmatic metaphor, the perfectly calibrated musical factory, its synchronized workforce led from a high vantage by visionary men of action. The symphony, like the grand metropolitan boulevard, expressed its age's fascination with massed power. Orchestras were complemented by soloists, who were seen as sentimental geniuses, projecting their lonely heroism from behind the footlights. Their emotional transports alone on stage bespoke the anxiety and alienation of the individual man and woman, who sensed that their traditional identities as members of small communities were being lost to the new society.

To feed their audiences' appetites for the sounds of armies and of lone wanderers, late-nineteenth-century composers composed grand opera and equally grand symphonies and concertos, and, at the other extreme, works for solo piano. To many composers, chamber music was of little more than technical interest. This was especially true of the German school, which dominated the musical landscape. Franz Liszt, Richard Wagner, Anton Bruckner, and Gustav Mahler composed little chamber music, and no string quartets at all. Several other European composers — Edward Elgar, Giuseppe Verdi, César Franck, Giacomo Puccini, and Claude Debussy — wrote one string quartet and, having proved that they could do it, made no further attempt. Verdi bragged that he wrote his E minor quartet merely to kill time in a hotel room while waiting out the postponement of a rehearsal.

During the latter half of the nineteenth century, the quartet was kept alive in two conservative camps: by composers and performers who wanted to temper their Romanticism with the old classicism, and by musicians who were independent of the German school. Brahms, the great classicist among the German Romantics, devoted lifelong attention to chamber music. Even he found the string quartet confining; his three quartets are so densely scored that they sound like reductions from symphonies. But when his chamber works include piano, which was his own instrument as a performer, they rival Mozart's and Beethoven's. Brahms's interest in chamber forms was shared more widely by composers outside of Austria and Germany. In Russia, Pyotr Tchaikovsky wrote three quartets, and in Bohemia, Dvořák, who was a performing string player, wrote fourteen. Tchaikovsky's quartets are superb — as good or better than Brahms' — although, unfortunately, they are not performed frequently. His three, Debussy's one, Brahms' first, and Dvorak's last five quartets are, to my ears, the great quartets of the last half of the century.

The Quartet among the Modernists

After the First World War, bitter disillusionment with industrial progress and mass society changed the direction of every European art. In music, composers returned to quartets and to other chamber forms. Almost unanimously, they saw the need for thoughtful music to move away from public declarations, made before audiences of thousands, towards the private ruminations and interpersonal explorations appropriate to small ensembles playing in intimate halls. Of the men who came to dominate the composition of new music after 1918, Arnold Schoenberg published four string quartets, and his pupils Anton Webern and Alban Berg published five between them. Sergey Prokofiev, Ralph Vaughan Williams, Jean Sibelius, Leos Janácek, and Charles Ives wrote two quartets each, Benjamin Britten three, Ernest Bloch five, Béla Bartók six, Paul Hindemith seven, Dmitri Shostakovich fifteen, Heitor Villa-Lobos seventeen, and Darius Milhaud eighteen.

When we consider the sea-change that these modernist composers brought to classical music, we tend to think of their rejection of traditional harmony and their adoption of alternatives to the major and minor modes. But their return to chamber music was a change in direction of no less significance. Once again, music lovers had the chance to contemplate, through the medium of their art, the virtues of family, teamwork, and friendship as antidotes to isolation and to submersion in the mass. A hundred years ago, it was acceptable for composers to ignore chamber music, and unthinkable for them to ignore the symphony. Nowadays, it is as viable for an artist of such stature as Murray Schafer to declare the orchestra obsolete[16] as it was for an artist of Gustav Mahler's stature to write for almost nothing else.

When modernist composers began testing alternatives to traditional harmony and tonality, they turned to the laboratory of chamber music, including string quartets, to run their musical experiments, just as Haydn, Mozart, and Beethoven had done. For a composer, the quartet is both simple and complex: simple because there are only four voices, whose sound-colors are very similar, and complex because of the infinity of possible combinations of melody and harmony as the four voices interweave. Quartets have both the purity and the open-endedness that are needed in a laboratory. For this reason, the quartet in the modern period once again attracted composers' boldest thoughts. As a result, some of the most beautiful and most challenging music written in this century has been composed for quartet. The quartets of an Austrian, a Hungarian, an Englishman, and a Russian — the four published by Schoenberg, the six by Bartók, the three by Britten, and the fifteen by Shostakovich — are among the masterworks of twentieth-century art.

The Quartet in the Electronic Age

Now, at the end of our century, almost all composers are ambitious to write for string quartet. Although their other creative choices may have little else in common, they agree on the irresistibility of this form. Murray Schafer, for example, who is best known for large works of musical theater, is also known for his six string quartets. He told an interviewer in 1991,

> It is a medium that is expressive in itself. There's so much in the way of dynamics that's possible with a quartet; the range is incredible. The types of attack are much more numerous than with other instruments. You can suggest incredible excitement with string instruments, you can express wonderful calm and serenity, and a lot of expressionism which isn't available with other instruments.[17]

Sydney Hodkinson, the Canadian-American conductor and composer, has written four quartets as well as a great deal of music for orchestra:

> The history of those four strings is fervent testimony to what one can do with the quartet. It's just made to order: the homogeneity among the instruments, the timbres, and all the counterpoint — it's compositionally an incredibly rich source of malleable musical stuff. You can get a dynamic range in a string quartet that you cannot get, for example, in a wind or brass quintet, particularly at the lower levels. There's an allowance for an intimacy, a most personal ambiance,

that is more difficult to feel in other media. The medium is so enticing because it's just four folks conversing together, sometimes in unison and sometimes arguing, just like all human relations.[18]

The American composer Terry Riley is a pioneer in minimalist music, in the world-music movement, and in the cross-over styles that merge classical music, rock, and jazz,. Before writing his nine string quartets, Riley studied the music of North India for ten years:

The quartet is traditionally a form in which the musicians work closely to develop a very high sense of music's purpose, which, as far as I'm concerned, is to bring you to a heightened state of awareness. For me, I wasn't working necessarily in the Western tradition and didn't want to be influenced by it when I was writing my quartets. I wanted to bring in a lot of the thinking that I felt was more related to the Eastern view of ensemble playing. So in the quartets I wrote for Kronos, you'll hear a lot of unison playing, and a lot of intricate rhythmic relationships.[19]

The American composer Martin Bresnick has written three quartets, as well as much other chamber music:

The string quartet can be a repository for abstract musical reflections. It can be connected to literary ideas. It's also open to dances, narratives, and other elements. My second quartet, entitled "Bucephalus," is picaresque, a series of episodes concerning a single character, although the meaning of the music is not exhausted by the story; it's also full of musical meanings. My third quartet, which is more personal, was inspired by the opening line of the *Inferno.* [20]

The continuing health of the quartet, and of chamber music in general, has been aided by the advent of recordings. String quartets can never rival the glorious noise of a hundred-piece orchestra pounding the ear in a concert hall, but on recordings the orchestra's sound is miniaturized and dimmed. The four voices of a quartet, on the other hand, can be heard more clearly between the stereo earphones than in many halls. The sound is simpler to begin with — the voices few, the colors spare. Further, stringed instruments, including the guitar, are less distorted by electronic repackaging than are many other instruments. The guitar would not, perhaps, have become the most important harmonic instrument in popular music if it did not lend itself to faithful electronic re-creation. Similarly, a quartet on a compact disk sounds much closer to its live original than a symphony and an opera to their originals. Even a piano solo almost always sounds pinched and reduced on recordings.

Besides, the beauty of much twentieth-century music — not only quartets — appears from behind its curtain of dissonant harmony and angular melody only after repeated hearings, which are rarely possible in a concert hall. Many of the older quartets, too — especially those of Schubert and Beethoven — are reluctant to reveal themselves with just one listening. But one can play a recording of a difficult piece as often as one wants, until the beauty of every phrase has become familiar. Modernist music is much more easily approached on recordings than in concert, simply because it can be approached repeatedly. Any listener can now study a piece of music with an intensity that, in the past, only performers would have the time and the skill to attain. For this reason, it is safe to say that, without the recording industry, twentieth-century classical music would never have gained the acceptance among audiences that it has long deserved and has finally achieved.

Concerts are public events, but we listen to recordings mostly in private. This difference between the two mediums also favors quartets. Composers have long followed Beethoven's choice of the quartet as a medium for the expression of intimate thoughts. The bareness of the four string voices are at the farthest remove from the riotous public chorus of orchestral colors. The quartet is more ascetic and more subtle — again Beethoven's discovery — even than the solo piano. Better than any other musical form, the quartet is suited to private expressions meant for private listening at home. On a recording — with the translating performers invisible — quartets seem to speak directly from the composer's soul.

The suitability of the quartet to recorded sound has ensured its survival in the electronic age in yet another way. Quartets are an obvious choice for musicians who employ recording technology as a medium of composition and performance. *Different Trains*, for example, a beautiful piece by the American minimalist Steve Reich, is scored for recorded train whistles, melodious fragments of recorded speech, and string quartet dubbed over itself three times.[21] The German modernist Karl Stockhausen has staged a work for helicopter and string quartet; the quartet broadcasts its four voices from aloft, amidst the helicopter's drone, while the composer, on the ground, manipulates the broadcast electronically.

Not only composers, but performers, too, have brought recording technology to live string quartet performance. The Kronos Quartet routinely plays with microphones attached to their traditional acoustic instruments, so that the audience hears the amplified sound. The Turtle Island String Quartet has gone a step further: it performs its jazz concerts on electric instruments, which do away with the 450-year old wooden soundbox altogether and pipe the strings' vibrations directly to the amplifier, in the manner of an electric guitar.

Pop music, of course, has grown up with the recording industry, and many pop performers now assemble their compositions in the studio. In such a case, there is no embarrassment in sneaking classical instruments into the mix — including the string quartet. The Beatles, pop's great classicists, were innovators in this furtive importation, as in so much else. The group made its first recording with a string quartet as backup in 1965, for the song "Yesterday." Paul McCartney's famous "Eleanor Rigby" is scored for tenor voice and double string quartet, without other accompaniment.[22] The group tipped its hand in its animated film *The Yellow Submarine*. In the film, four string quartet players represent the musical civilization that has been devastated by the music-hating Blue Meanies. It is the elderly cellist who guides the young pop band to their timely escape and welcomes them on their heroic return. More recently, the British vocalist Elvis Costello has brought the string quartet out of the pop studio and onto the stage, collaborating with the Brodsky Quartet in a song cycle for tenor and string quartet, *The Juliet Letters*.[23]

The Four and the One

When Beethoven began composing, it had by no means been determined that the consort of violins would be scored for four instruments only. Luigi Boccherini, who was writing quartets at the same time as Haydn, was also writing quintets, for five stringed instruments: two violins, one viola, and two cellos. Mozart wrote six "viola quintets," as they are now called, for two violins, one cello, and two violas. Two among them, those in G minor and C major, are superior to his quartets. Many other composers of the time wrote string quintets. In confining himself to quartets, Haydn was the exception. But after writing five string trios and one viola quintet in his twenties, Beethoven followed Haydn and wrote quartets only. It was he who made the decision — so authoritatively that no one since has thought to revise it — that the dominant chamber ensemble of strings would after all be the quartet. He was the arbiter who focused the future of chamber music on the peculiar tension that is created when four people, and four voices, are joined.

The size of an ensemble of instruments makes a profound difference in the nature of the music. A group of three consists of a middle and two extremes. In music, the obvious scoring for a threesome is for a high instrument, a low instrument, and one in between. But a group of three voices is too small to create a convincing group sound. When we listen to string trios, for example, we can hear all three instruments clearly throughout. The ear is continually aware of the violin with the tune on top, the cello sawing the bass, the viola filling in the middle. Most of the time, a trio does not sound like a bonded group; what we hear are three individuals who happen to be playing together. They are three, but they do not become one.

Later composers have agreed with Beethoven that, if three voices are what one wants, it makes far more sense to score the three for piano trio — for piano, violin, and cello — rather than for violin, cello, and viola. In the piano trio, the contrast between the instruments is brought forward. The music accepts and exploits the separation in sound that unavoidably exists between

29

voices when there are only three of them. The piano, meanwhile, fills in the harmony with its multiple tones.

A group of five members, on the other hand, is too complex to grasp with a single glance of the eye or ear. We can see and hear the whole group, but we cannot hear clearly, or even focus our eyes on, each of the individuals in a group of five at the same moment. While it is hard for a threesome to merge into one, then, it is even harder for a group of five to remain distinct as individuals. They are easily joined into one, but they cannot be separately five. Our senses have to simplify an assemblage of five by dividing it in two parts — into sections of three members and two members, or occasionally into one and four. In Mozart's viola quintets, for example, the first violin and first viola are soloists playing opposite one another, each grouped with a shifting balance of accompanists. Thus, while the sound of a trio is too thin to make a fully blended sound, the sound of quintet is already heavy enough in texture to cloak the individual lines.

But in a human foursome, and in a string quartet, the group and all its individual members are present to the senses at the same time. Listening to quartets, it takes professional ears, or, for an amateur, the utmost concentration, to hear just what all four voices are saying at any one moment. Yet we are always aware of the presence of the four, even as they are joined in a group sound. They are separate and at the same time merged; we cannot say whether they are four or one, because they are both. Thus the number four represents most effectively the nature of the small human group. It summarizes the paradox of the one and the many which is at the basis of the human condition. We are social beings, and we are individual souls. We are alone, and we are also together. In this paradox lies the power of the string quartet.

2. Playing Roles

Introduction

In the center of Ann Elliott-Goldschmid's studio, the Lafayette Quartet is sitting in rehearsal. Sheet music, purses, lunches in plastic bags, and open stringed-instrument cases with maroon plush innards lie strewn about the floor. The telephone is shut off, the corridor outside the door is silent. The quartet's students at the University of Victoria School of Music in British Columbia have scattered for the summer. Beyond the studio window, the drone of a leaf-blower tidying the rhododendron beds is the only disturbance on campus. For the next two weeks, the musicians have kept concerts off their schedule. They are free to devote day-long rehearsals to learning new repertoire — a once-a-year luxury.

For rehearsal, the members of the quartet have placed themselves along three sides of a rectangle. Ann, on first violin, and Pam Highbaugh, on cello, face each other over their music stands, while Sharon Stanis and Joanna Hood, on second violin and viola, sit side by side between the others:

Sharon   *Joanna*

Ann   *Pam*

As for myself, I'm sitting as far back in a corner as Ann's grand piano will permit me, so that I'm out of the players' lines of sight. A half-sized booklet — a miniature score — is open on the closed keyboard in front of me. It is Alexander Borodin's Quartet No. 2, the most widely performed Russian quartet from the nineteenth century. The Lafayette rehearsed the first two movements yesterday, and today they'll begin with the third movement — the famous "Notturno," or "night-song."

The four members of the Lafayette are nearly the same age — thirty-three or thirty-four — and, except Sharon, a little above middle height. Little else about them is similar either in appearance or temperament, beyond the expressive vitality and the devotion to work that are occupational necessities for all musicians. Ann's wide mouth smiles often, with an effusive friendliness that hints at the characteristics common to many first violinists. In quartets, the first violin is most often the lead voice, and the performer who plays the lead tends to be the one who loves the spotlight. There's a shyness in Ann's brown eyes, though, that doesn't suggest a soloist eager for display. She keeps her straight brown hair cut short, and for rehearsal today she's wearing wire-rimmed glasses, black tights, and a long loose orange sweater to accommodate her four months' pregnancy. Ann is from New Brunswick — the only Canadian-born member of the quartet.

The group has begun the morning by playing through the third movement of the Borodin for the first time as a quartet. As Ann plays, she tucks her feet beneath her chair, alternately hunches forward, tips back so that she's not quite facing the ceiling, then straightens, then rises off her chair so that she's half standing. Throughout the movement, she holds her lips inward to catch them between her teeth. At the end she shakes her head, muttering, "I've got to warm up."

Sharon is from Cleveland, of a Polish-American background, although her face suggests a touch of Romany. Her features would not seem foreign in northern India. The bridge of her nose falls straight from her brows, and a strong upward comma curls over her nostrils. This summer, she's wearing her dark hair cut shaggy to shoulder length, and, today, a black short sleeved jersey above a beige pleated skirt. She holds her instrument higher along her jaw than most violinists, partly against her cheek, with her head tipped against it as if she were listening to its insides. While playing, Sharon's movements suggest none of the mildness or self-effacement that belong to the tradition of second violinists. She is instead the most demonstrative of her colleagues, the one most likely to shout or to clown. During the third movement of the Borodin, she thrusts out her feet to rest them on the points of her shoe-heels; she raises her eyebrows, rounds her black eyes, drops her chin to make an O with her mouth. In the second section of the movement, as the two violins exchange a new melody, Sharon lifts off her chair with Ann and remains half standing till the cello's opening melody returns.

The cello has begun the movement with a celebrated love-song. The aria descends in a series of downward sighing fourths through two and a half octaves of the cello's range. The sound is unmistakably amorous. When Robert Wright and George Forrest drew on Alexander Borodin's melodies to create the 1952 Broadway musical *Kismet*, this was the melody they chose for the hero and heroine to make their declaration of love.[24] In the musical, the cello's solo became "This is My Beloved." It begins:

When quartet music is written down, the four musical lines are arranged according to pitch. Thus the notes played by the first violin, normally the highest voice, are written on the top line, the second violin's notes on the second line, the viola on the third line, and last the cello's notes along the bottom. Here, in the example, the first violin is silent — marked by rests on the top line — while the aria for cello is written on the fourth line. The second violin and the viola, on the two middle lines, play pulsing, off-the-beat chords to accompany the cello. The second violin, on the second line, is playing two notes, on two strings — what string-players call a double-stop. The music moves through time horizontally from left to right on the page, while the four instruments sound together at each vertical moment. Most people can't read off four lines of music silently and hear them all combined in their heads — I certainly can't. But the up-and-down contour of the cello melody, and the repetitions of the accompanying chords, hint to the eye what the ear hears in performance — the strands of the individual voices as they weave a pattern of concerted sound.

As she plays her solo, Pam doesn't shift her feet or rise off her chair like her violinist colleagues. She stays at anchor with a straight back. She sometimes tips or tosses her head to the right, and occasionally allows herself a side-to-side sway. Today she's wearing a green sleeveless top and a long print skirt that accommodates her instrument between her knees. As her solo melody in the Borodin descends from tenor notes deep into the bass, her spidery fingers stalk up the fingerboard in wide-legged steps.

A California softness in Pam's blue eyes is balanced by a determined chin, towards which her red hair sweeps along her jawline. Her contrasting features, suggesting gentleness and firmness, fit the contrast of roles of her instrument. Sometimes in quartets, as in Borodin's Notturno, the cello in quartet sings an emotional aria. More often it establishes the harmonies and disciplines the rhythms as it lays down the notes of the bass.

The cello's declaration of love, twenty-three measures long, is finally answered by the first violin. Its soprano voice repeats the melody two octaves higher. The gesture strikes the ear immediately as a lover's reply. As Ann begins her turn with the melody, she is immediately joined by an unexpected voice — a counter-melody in the lowest baritone range of the viola. It caressingly weaves and winds around the aria in the violin.

In the example, the first violin, on the top line, repeats the cello melody note for note. The viola, on the third line, is playing the sinuous counter-melody. The second violin and the cello are meanwhile holding down accompanying chords, with the second violin again playing double-stops.

Joanna's 1607 Amati is an alto viola, with a wooden body about sixteen inches long.[24a] But even on the larger tenor violas, the relatively mild resonance of the lower strings tends to understate a deep-voiced melody like this one in Borodin's night-song. The sound can submerge beneath the cello and the violins. For viola solos, composers of quartets often go out of their way to subdue the other three instruments. They may direct the cellist and the violinists to pluck their strings instead of bow them, or else to damp them with mutes, while the violist bows freely.[25] The viola's voice is even less easily heard when it is given a countermelody against a violin, as here in the Borodin. Most performing ensembles leave this viola line buried within the sound — treating it simply as part of the accompaniment.

Faced with the impediments built into their instruments, successful violists need the tenacity to insist that their colleagues tone down their more resonant instruments to let their solos through. They also need a temperament of detachment, which can accept that their voice will always be the least penetrating in the ensemble. The old stigma, too — that the viola is the refuge of the least competent players — still stings, even though it hasn't been true for several generations. For all these reasons, the viola attracts skeptics, ironists, and humorists. Some violists delight in an endemic self-deprecatory genre, the viola-joke:

A violist comes home after a symphony concert and finds his house burned to the ground. The fire chief approaches him. "I'm very sorry, sir. Everything's been lost. Your wife, your children, everything. And we know who did it. It was the conductor of the symphony."

Violist (overjoyed): "You mean the maestro came to *my house?*"26

Joanna, though not a joke-teller, is an expert placer of the dry remark. Among her colleagues, she is the most laconic and reserved. She merely says, "I tend to be more objective than the others."

The viola is, besides, an awkward artifact, even more so than the violin and the cello. Like the violin, the viola must be held firmly in an unnatural grip between the chin and the left shoulder. In order to change the pitches by pressing down the strings against the fingerboard, violists and violinists have to turn their left hands around backwards. The viola is made yet more cumbersome than the violin by its greater length and weight. Violists therefore need strong backs and long arms. Joanna plays with her shoulders slightly hunched forward, to add more reach.

For the rehearsal today, she's wearing a blue T-shirt and a long flower-print skirt. She has left her long straight blond hair unbraided, and when the music allows her a rest, she tips back her head to shake her hair behind her ears. She has a round face, with high cheekbones and dark blue eyes. She's the least likely of the four to transmit the emotions of the music into physical gestures and facial expressions. She holds her straight mouth firmly shut as she plays, and the tension in the music appears only in a series of wrinkles which gather and smooth again across the full width of her brow.

Joanna is a native of Seattle, across the water from Vancouver Island. Thus she was the only member of the Lafayette Quartet to return nearly home when, after several years of struggle, the

young ensemble won competitions, signed a contract with a recording label, enlisted a national manager, booked international
tours, and landed a faculty appointment here in Victoria.

Critique

The last notes of the Notturno — an ecstatic, dreamy A-
major chord — are silent in the studio. The four players sit quietly for a minute, considering. Each musician is reluctant to claim
too quickly the first word in a critique. Ann has lowered her
hands to her knees, leaving her violin pointing out from her
neck, clamped between shoulder and chin. In discussion, she'll
sometimes punctuate with her bow. Sharon has propped her
right elbow on her knee and her chin on her right hand. Her left
hand, curled around her violin's neck, stands the instrument on
her other knee. Pam slants her cello to the right to rest against
her leg. She holds her bow in her right hand, parallel to the
strings, leaving her left hand free to gesture. Joanna lays her
viola sidewise, strings facing outward, across her lap.

Sharon, finally, begins with a comment on the first restate-
ment of the love song, where the viola's weaving countermelody
sounds against the aria in the first violin. The notes, again, look
like this in the score — first violin on top with the melody, viola
on the third line with the countermelody:

"When the viola enters," Sharon says, "I want the emotional priorities to be Joanna's voice first, then Ann's, then Pam's and mine. Right now, it feels like Ann's voice is strongest, then Pam's and mine, then Joanna's last."

Sharon's colleagues are surprised that the viola line might sound best as the strongest voice — as more important, even, than the melody in the violin. That's not how it's usually performed. "You're kidding," Ann says, intrigued. Without further comment, the quartet plays through the section again. Joanna, though louder now, doesn't yet sound like the soloist Sharon has proposed. When they put down their bows, Sharon suggests that her colleagues help Joanna by "getting out of her way" — by dropping down in their own volume.

"There should be half the sound on the second violin and cello accompaniment," she says. "It should be a most intimate moment when the baritone comes in." To illustrate her sense of the moment's mood as expressed by the caressive countermelody, Sharon reaches across with her right hand to caress her own left shoulder. "It's someone's fingers all around you."

Ann laughs in agreement. "It's such a great love scene. It's so thick."

The quartet plays the passage a third time, and now the viola's melody can be heard clearly beneath the violin's, embracing the violin aria as it soars. "A bit too much, I'd say," Ann remarks.

Sharon disagrees: "I loved the balance."

The others nod and raise their bows for the next passage. There's no vote on Sharon's proposal, no further comment. It's understood that they'll try it her way next time, and see what they think then. They need to move on, since every passage in the movement will require similar scrutiny.

The discussion was typical of quartet rehearsals. The melodies, in this case, belonged to the first violin and the viola; but someone else — the second violinist — took the lead in the critique. In an orchestra, by contrast, there would be no call on Sharon to advance her view of the best musical interpretation of a piece. How loudly the first violins and violas should play their parts against each other in a symphony would be none of her business, even if she were one of the people playing. The conductor would give instructions, and the players would follow without argument. Discussion would be superfluous. In the opposite case, if Sharon were a soloist playing a concerto, the accompanying orchestra would follow her, also without argument, after she had decided how to phrase her melodies herself. But in a string quartet, there is neither soloist nor conductor. How the volume should balance between the instruments, and every other subtlety of a subtle art, has to be investigated by the quartet as a team.

A few minutes later, the quartet returns to the beginning of the movement, and now Ann begins the critique — even though, at that point, she is the only one who isn't playing. To repeat the example:

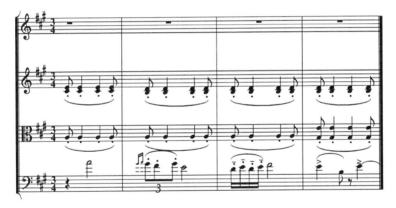

Since the composer built the accompaniment in chords of three notes, he could easily have given the top note to the first violin. Instead, he kept the first violin silent (marked by rests on the top line), and required the second violin, on the second line, to fill in two of the notes in double-stops. The viola plays the lowest note of the chord, while the cello, on the bottom line, sings above them all. The first violin seems to be acting the role of the beloved who is listening quietly to her lover's declaration as it is spoken by the cello.

As I myself listen from my corner, I'm expecting Ann to critique Pam's interpretation of the cello solo. The famous melody is what the quartet's audiences will be listening for. Besides, in a moment Ann will be playing the melody herself, and she might well be tempted to urge Pam to begin it the way *she'd* like to continue it.

Instead, Ann zeroes in on the pulsing accompaniment. She tells Sharon and Joanna, "You're crescendoing on each chord" — creating little swells on each beat.

Joanna shakes her head. "No. I don't want that."

Joanna and Sharon, without Pam, repeat the opening chords, playing them more evenly. Ann says, "Right, it's there, but don't accent them."

They begin again, and Pam joins in with her solo. But Ann calls out after a few measures: "That's nicer, but" —

The other musicians make a halt, which Sharon punctuates with a loud upward glissando slide on her high E-string: *Zooop!*

Ann continues, "But there's still to much of a beginning about the sound" — too much of an accent. "Do it so the instrument's ringing, but you're not causing it to ring, you don't hear the bow playing it."

Again they begin, but this time Pam interrupts with a new consideration. "I think the tempo should be a little more staid."

Sharon, incredulous: "Staid?"

"More steady. Every time, I've felt pushed through the sixteenth notes." To demonstrate what she'd like to hear, Pam sings these faster notes in the third measure of her solo gently and steadily, free from the impetus of an accompaniment that seemed to her rushed.

Joanna: "Yeah. Okay."

Resuming, the accompanists play almost without accent, and more slowly, creating a background that's gentle and steady in sound, at once languid and intense in mood.

But Joanna is unhappy with the slower tempo. "You know, I'm thinking we're too ... we're too ... lugubrious."

Sharon laughs. "Well, in that case —"

Joanna asks Pam: "Didn't you feel we were holding you back?" — by playing too slowly.

"I liked it, but" —

Sharon says, "Well, we'll follow what you do."

40

Musicians who play together must coordinate their timing, as the members of the Lafayette are struggling to do, but they cannot make things simple by firmly deciding on a specific, steady speed. To keep strict time together by thumping regularly on the downbeat, or else regularly off the beat, like guitarists in a rock band, will not answer for Borodin's caressive lovesong. Much of the emotional expressiveness of music is achieved through deliberate delays or accelerations in the timing, usually of tenths or hundredths of a second. As accompanists, Sharon and Joanna will need to learn where in her aria Pam intends to accelerate and delay.

The three musicians play again from the beginning. Sharon and Joanna hold their instruments high and look over them at Pam, to follow her bow and so learn her timing more easily. Pam plays slightly faster, but with languishing delays.

Ann, meanwhile, is still not happy with the quality of the accompaniment's sound. She tells Sharon and Joanna, "You're each very different, how you're playing this." She pauses, and Sharon, perhaps a shade nettled, prods: "So what's your—"

Joanna steps in to soften Ann's criticism. "I think it's so much easier for me because I don't have the double stops most of the time, so I feel like for me it's easier to get a cushiony, soft—"

Her voice trails off, and Ann presses on: "I like what you're doing with your downbow. But at the end of your upbow there's still kind of a *yee*-dum-dum." She's talking about the change in directions, from down to up, in Sharon's bowstroke. To Ann's ears, Sharon's sound is changing too audibly with the direction of her bow. On her own violin, Ann plays Sharon's double-stopped thirds with a pulse on the upbow, to demonstrate what she doesn't like hearing. "But I like the separation you're getting between the chords. Maybe try once a dry kind of, like a woodwind kind of sound?"

Sharon: "Mm. Sure."

She and Joanna play their first two chords, before the entrance of the cello with its solo. Joanna interrupts: "I feel like the first chord should be" — she plays it separated and slightly delayed from the second chord.

Ann: "Yes. Exactly."

Joanna: "And Pam can come off of it whenever she wants."

They raise their bows to begin again. Pam asks: "Faster? Slower?"

Ann: "Let's try it a little faster. Then they can push against you." They begin, but in a moment Ann interrupts with still another consideration — intonation. She turns to Joanna. "You're out of tune." One note in the opening chord had been very slightly flat — imperceptibly to any but professional ears. The players begin again, and Ann interrupts again: "Faster?"

They play through Pam's solo as Ann listens. Afterward, she says to the two accompanists: "That was a lot better in terms of matched sound. You're almost exactly together now. So it sounds like one instrument now, doing maybe not exactly the right thing, but exactly the same bow stroke, and that's the key."

From soundmaking, timing, and intonation, Joanna next turns the discussion to a fourth concern, that of balance in volume between the accompaniment and the melody. She feels that the accompaniment, in reaching for subtlety and gentleness, has become too quiet in comparison with the aria. Perhaps the solo should be toned down. "Pam, you don't have to put out quite as much sound as you have been. Or, we could play out more, because I feel a big difference between what you're putting out and what we're doing."

Sharon: "I don't even mind Pam being more out, like a soloist, but I'm feeling so distant from it, sort of detached."

But Ann liked the balance. "In a way, you guys should be more a little, just, oom-pah-pah sisters, not feeling like it's your story." To Pam, she adds merely, "Can I just say one thing? I thought your solo was gorgeous. There were only a couple of places where I thought you might have gone a little too much out of the realm of a crescendo than you needed to go. And when you're going *taa*-dum" — she sings the melody's characteristic sighing downward fourth — "be careful you don't drop your sound on the second note below what you need so you can do something with it."

Pam: "Right."

Equal and Different

Ann's few words are all the appraisal Pam is to hear today of her playing of the love song. The entire critique of the first part of the movement has concerned the accompanying chords. But that is not due to a consensus that Pam has been playing her aria better than Sharon and Joanna have been playing their simple background notes. Rather, their accompanying chords are actually as difficult to play well as the melody, and they are no less crucial to the music. To play the lead voice in a performance, of course, requires technical mastery, emotional range, and hardened nerves. A melody is more exposed than an accompaniment, and it draws the attention of the audience. But what the audience is actually hearing is the melody in the context of the other voices. The accompaniment sets in place the musical building blocks on which the melody stands, and without them the melody would collapse.

In the first place, for Pam's aria in Borodin's Notturno, the accompanying chords establish the rhythmic pulse within which the melody moves. The chords also provide the harmony, which must be perfectly in tune; without harmony, the melody would be ambiguous, if not meaningless, and much of its beauty would be lost. Third, the accompaniment must create the appropriate quality of background sound to set the mood for the song. Finally, the accompanists must support the melodist with exactly the right balance of volume, so that the melody sounds neither cloaked nor bare. Timing, soundmaking, balance, and perfect tuning of the harmony: each of these considerations was discussed in turn during the Lafayette's critique.

Players in an orchestra are almost always embedded in a mass of sound, even when they are playing the melody. But in a quartet, every voice is exposed, even when it is sounding in the middle of a chord. No voice in quartet is merely supplementary, added for a touch of color or for a slightly richer sonority, as players or singers are added to orchestras and choruses. If no one in town plays the contrabassoon, a local orchestra can stage the concert anyway; but if a member of a quartet is missing, the concert is canceled — or else the remaining performers remember their string trios. Whether accompanying or playing the melody, then, every part in a quartet is equally indispensable. One of the reasons that the string quartet has drawn the best efforts of so many composers during more than two centuries is the challenge it poses: to realize the full effect of the form, every note, like every word in a poem, must count.

The challenge is made greater by the similarity among the instruments' sounds. The string quartet does not offer the wind ensemble's pleasing color contrasts. The violin, viola, and cello sound more alike even than the bass, tenor, contralto, and soprano registers of the human voice; in a way, the three stringed instruments are the same instrument, like the various registers of a piano. Further, the cello, viola, and violin are tuned in an overlapping progression, so that they share many of their notes. The lowest quartet string, on the cello, is tuned to the second C below middle C. The cello's higher strings follow, in fifths, at G, D, and A.

The viola is tuned exactly an octave above the cello, proceeding from the first C below middle C to the succeeding G, D, and A.

Because the viola's open tunings bridge the bass and treble clefs, viola parts are written instead on the alto clef — also called the C clef, since middle C is placed on the middle line of the staff. These are the viola tunings again, on the alto clef:

For their part, the two violins begin at the G below middle C, followed by D, A, and E.

44

Thus the open strings of the three different instruments are tuned only to C, G, D, A, and E. They step well into each other's territory, too: the cello's highest string sounds one whole-step above the violin's lowest string. As for the viola in the middle, it not only repeats the cello's tunings an octave higher but shares three of its tunings with the violins.

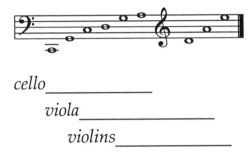

*cello*_____

*viola*_____

*violins*_____

And, of course, the two higher instruments, the first and second violins, are the same. In quartets, the two violins are distinguishable in their sound chiefly in that the second violinist, as the mezzo-soprano voice and sometimes the alto voice, spends most of her time playing on her three lower strings, while her colleague soars above her on the high E-string.

Still, the quartet's sixteen strings are not a seamless weave. Because they differ in size, the violin, viola, and cello do not all resonate in the same way, and are therefore distinguishable by the ear, even when they are playing the same note. The quartet, then, whatever music is written for it, is built inevitably on a contradiction. It consists of four instruments which sound like one instrument, at the same time that they sound like four. This is why quartets can embody, more exactly than any other musical form, the intrinsic duality of human relations. Each member plays a distinct role in the shared work of creating a whole. Players of quartets are engaged in, and their listeners are hearing, a constant circling through a paradox of separateness and unity.

To say that the four quartet instruments, and the four musicians who play them, fill equally indispensable roles, does not
mean that their roles are the same. Their parts differ because
their instruments differ in pitch. That the first violin plays high,
the cello low, and the other two instruments in the middle sub-
jects them to the preferences of the human ear. We hear higher
sound frequencies as salient. In a countryside in spring, what
stands out is birdsong; in a house, the cries of children. To make
a melody heard, then, musicians usually cast it in the highest
among the voices that are sounding at the moment. In string
quartets, that is usually the first violin. To place the melody elsewhere, in a lower voice, as with Borodin's cello aria, is to offer
an exception that by itself becomes a matter of aesthetic interest
to listener and performer. And a lower voice with a melody must
usually rise to its upper register to be heard above the accompaniment — the cello moves to its high A-string, the baritone singer
climbs to the notes he shares with tenors. This gravitation of
melody to a relatively high pitch is a principle that applies to
music generally, to Western and non-Western traditions alike.[27]

Similarly, in establishing the foundation of the harmony,
the cello in quartets plays the role that belongs to the bass in
almost any musical ensemble. In listening to Western harmonic
music, the ear is most satisfied by hearing the home-note of a
chord sounded at the bottom. In the same way, in the musics of
North and South India, the home-note of a melody is repeated
throughout a song by means of a drone. The drone is maintained
by a stringed instrument or tuned drum below the melody, not
above it.[28] Finally, with the tonal basis grounded on the bottom
and the tune flirting about on the top, the other instruments,
whatever they may be, fill in the texture of the sound in the only
place left, which is the middle. This is why, in quartets, the second violin and viola end up, most often, with the accompaniment.

Some writers of string quartets — the American composer
Elliott Carter, for example — have used the quartet as a con-
struction site for dismantling the pitch-determined roles of instruments and for rebuilding them so that they are not only
equally important but almost interchangeable. Discarding the

traditional assignments of melody to high instruments and harmony to low ones is more natural to modernist music, like Carter's, which departs from traditional melody and harmony in the first place. But most quartet composers have, instead, seen the traditional pitch-roles as a pattern to preserve and at the same time work against. Their quartets become structures of criss-crossing members as the instruments move in and out of their ordinary places. Thus at the opening of Borodin's Notturno, the cello plays the highest note, the viola sets the harmonic foundation on its baritone C-string, the second violin fills in the chord, and the first violin is silent. Then the viola switches to a countermelody against the aria in the first violin, while the cello moves to bass and the second violin continues in the middle with double-stops. In the next passage, the two violins exchange a new melody, phrase for phrase in the same register, while the cello continues the bass and the viola fills in the chord.

All this shifting back and forth enforces the equality of the voices and emphasizes the quartet paradox of separateness and unity, of four and one. As in most human groups, the role-boundaries are unstable and the responsibilities are in motion. As a result, the four quartet players must be matched in their musicianship. All must be able to call upon the depth, nerve, and technical skill of a soloist, and all must also exercise the accompanist's empathy and ability to listen and blend. They all need the agility to leap between the two roles of soloist and accompanist at a moment's notice, abruptly altering their volume and the quality of their sound — here "playing out" with a melody, there "getting out of the way" of a colleague. For this reason, of all the music for stringed instruments, quartets are the hardest to play.

In Their Words

The roles of their instruments was the subject of one of my first interviews with the members of the Lafayette. We spoke during a lunch break after the rehearsal of the Borodin.

Ann: Being able to play a Paganini Violin Concerto or some other virtuoso showpiece doesn't mean you can play quartets well. The Mozart quartets, for example, are not difficult technically for the first violin. Compared to all the things we violinists grow up learning, just to get a handle on the instrument, the Mozart quartets are not difficult at all, not even as hard as his violin concertos. But there's a finesse in the sound. Mozart is like thin glass. You put just a little too much weight, and you bury him. You can't overvibrate, you have to have a subtlety of tone and perfect intonation and an understanding of the complexity of the music that you don't need to have when you're playing a showpiece.

Kids, you know, they're always saying, "Oh, do we have to learn a *Mozart* quartet?" They think that it'll be too easy for them. But every single part in the Mozart quartets is interesting all by itself. The inner parts sound sometimes like twentieth-century music. I listen to Sharon's part in Beethoven sometimes, and it just blows my mind. So she's got to be listening to all the other parts in order to make any sense at all of hers. And we all have to do that. In quartet, you're not ever just playing your own line, ever, even when you have the melody. You're playing all the lines, every single time you play. And that's what's so fun. Every time I play, I'm thinking, yes, this is a beautiful melody, but what makes it beautiful is what the composer is doing with the harmonies underneath, how he moves them around.

Sharon: It's in the nature of the music for the first violinist to have more influence on how a phrase is turned. When we play Haydn and Mozart quartets, a big responsibility is on Ann to be imaginative, and my job is to swim around and make sure I can figure out how to enhance what she wants. I use the analogy all the time of two fish swimming. It has to be synchronized. Ann is taking a phrase somewhere, and when I have something with her, I'm trying to second guess what she wants.

Ann: Just to play the notes, the second violin part isn't as hard as the first violin part, except one sixteenth of the time. But Sharon's part is terribly hard, because she has to adjust to me. If I'm out of tune, she has to change with me. She's my net, and that's a terribly difficult position to be in.

Sharon: Even when I was a student, I loved playing the parts of the

48

second violin, and I wanted someone else to do the gymnastics on first violin on top of me. On second violin, I do get showcased, I play those solos when they come and I give them all I've got, but I don't have to worry about all the gymnastics. I sometimes think of playing an inner voice in a quartet as being in the trenches, not in a negative sense, but in the sense that you're there making sure of all the practicalities, like the eighth-note start that sets the pulse in the Notturno. You're setting the girding underneath – and oh, here's a little spotlight moment for me, just two measures – okay, now I'm back in the trenches, let's clean up, let's do a little sweeping. And meanwhile you're striving to make your own part gorgeous, like velvet, like a pearl.

Joanna: Being in the middle and being the only one of the viola, I definitely feel akin to both sides. But either way, the viola is an accompaniment instrument, basically. You do get solos, and that's always a special moment because of the color of the viola that people aren't used to hearing, but acoustically the viola is not as much in the forefront as a violin and it can definitely be swamped by a cello. So it's the inner voice which makes the harmony more complex and adds a darker color.

To play harmony in quartet was natural for me, because when I was a kid I used to love to listen to rock and roll all the time, and when I would sing along, which I always did, I would always sing the harmony, always, first because I could pick it out, and also because I could make my own. Or I would sing with my friends and they would sing the song and I would sing the harmony. I just enjoyed that. Once you got the melody, well, that was it, it was the melody, but finding the harmony was a lot more interesting.

A lot of times in earlier quartet music – and even in Bartók this is still how it is – the two upper voices will be paired against the two lower voices, so I'll be with the cello against the two violins. The other main option is the second violin joining with the viola to create the sound of the inner voices. Sometimes the viola is with the first violin and the second violin will pair with the cello, too, like the passage we were rehearsing in the Borodin, where the viola has the countermelody against the first violin, but that's the least common combination. Mainly it's the second violin with the viola. You just

49

look at any score and you'll see that. It's the same in a Bach chorale: it's more usually the bass voices working against the treble voices, while the inner voices work together in between . As you get into later music there's more freedom for the inner parts, but on viola, you're usually providing the harmony.

That's one reason why we sit the way we do, with Pam on the outside facing Ann, and Sharon and me in the middle. That puts me in a strategic spot, because I'm between Pam and Sharon, the two people I'm usually paired with. From an ensemble viewpoint, it's better for the inner voices to be in the middle.

second violin   *viola*

first violin   *cello*

The only drawback is that there's less of a connection between the viola and the first violin.

Ann: The diagonal connection is the hardest in quartet.

Joanna: Because I'm the farthest back, and I can't see Ann very well.

Ann: And I'm not projecting over to her.

Joanna: She can never play into me, because if she does, then the sound doesn't go to the audience.

Ann: Exactly.

Joanna: So I have to sort of imagine how she's sounding. Of course, a lot of quartets place the cello in the middle, instead of the viola, and their violist sits on the outside.

second violin   *cello*

first violin   *viola*

That allows the bass of the quartet, which is the cello, come from the middle of the group, and then the cello is facing straight out, which is better acoustically. That's how a cellist plays when she's playing a solo.

But the trouble there for a quartet is, if the violist is sitting on the outside, now the back of her instrument is facing the audience. A lot of violists who sit on the outside turn out to face the audience when they have a solo. Acoustically, the best place for the viola would be where the violins are, because then the face of the instrument would be projecting directly into the audience. But you don't want the viola to be in the forefront. You want it to be a more subtle ingredient in the mix.

Pam: On the cello, you don't get to fly away as much as the first violin. Usually you have the least flashy voice. It's actually hard to define the cello's role, and I think that even when I'm ninety, I probably won't feel I can satisfactorily say what it is. You're providing the bass that gives everything else its shape and marks the place that everything can embark from. It sets the tone for what the sound can be. I can interject character and energy, and sometimes the cello is a voice of reason, or a voice of humor. I enjoy that. I would really love to be in a rock band, and if I were, I would want to be the electric bass player. I like to be able to put down just one thing and get it to hold.

So my role as a cellist is to be really responsible, really grounded. And then all of a sudden you're the soloist, and then you are — not the most poignant voice, because there are so many poignant moments with the viola — but you're giving a color that no other instrument could begin to give. And those moments are what you love about the cello, because of the impact and the power and the range.

Usually, though, I'm not under the gun in the same way as Ann is. But that doesn't mean I don't have to put out as much, in terms of my understanding, as Ann has to when she's playing the melody. I don't view it that I have an easier job than she does, although maybe some other people feel that way, but I don't. How I put my energy into preparing to play in quartet is the same as I would to be a soloist.

3. Voices

The Bowed String

The basic technology of stringed instruments was discovered by prehistoric musicians. A string of gut or fiber, when stretched between two fixed points and plucked, will emit a tone. If the open length of the string is made shorter or stretched more tightly, the tone will be higher. By pinching the string, the player can easily control how much of its length is free to vibrate, and thus he can make the tone's pitch higher or lower at will. In other words, he can play a tune. The sound-quality of the tones can be varied, too, according to the material the string is made of, the manner in which the string is plucked, and the shape and composition of the amplification device. Prehistoric musicians amplified stretched strings by causing them to resonate in partly enclosed volumes of air. They made use of such containers as gourds, bark-covered holes in the ground, and the mouth (with one end of the string held between the teeth). By the beginning of historic times, these simple instruments had already been elaborated into lutes and harps.

But plucking a string can create vibrations only by a single, momentary contact between the string and the plectrum or finger. The sound is small, compared to a shout or a blast of a horn, and even if a plucked string's vibrations are strongly amplified, they soon die away. Strings' potential to make music remained cloaked, therefore, until the invention of the bow. The bow was apparently conceived by Middle Eastern musicians near the end of the first millennium A.D., and it entered Europe through Spain in the eleventh century.[29] It granted players three new capabilities. First, players could now sustain a tone, as harpists and lutenists cannot do. As a bow is drawn back and forth across a string for the upbow and downbow, it can continue to vibrate the string for as long as there is strength in the player's arm. Second, players can vary the loudness of a tone as they sustain it, by varying either the speed of the bow or its downward pressure on the string. Finally — and most magical — the bowed string can create so many variations in sound-quality that it can rival the subtle organ of communication that human beings evolved over millennia — the voice.

The violin family, especially, can imitate exactly most of the voice's pre-verbal expressions of emotion — the sob, the cry, the scream, the moan, the croon of pleasure, the snarl. It can imitate the communicative inflections we load our words with — the rising voice for a question, the falling voice for disappointment, the crescendoing voice for menace. By variations in the bowstroke — by how it moves across a string — it can produce vowels. By variations in the attack of the bow — by how it is made to meet a string — it can produce consonants. String players often describe the sound effects they seek in terms of phonemes.

Sharon: If I put down the bow for an Aaah, I don't hear the sound as clearly as a Daa. Which is different than a Yaa. Sometimes a Maa, if it's too mushy, has to be turned into a Baa. You go for a Maa but put a tiny bit of a Baa at the beginning to project the sound into the hall.

During the seventeenth century, violinmakers perfected the art of shaping and shaving the top plates and back plates of violins and cellos so that the wood resonated sympathetically with the open strings. The result was an amplification device of unprecedented power. The bowed stringed instrument's sound could now equal, for the first time, the range, power, and flexibility of the best trained singer. In its expressiveness, it imitated the inflections of the voice, but — like other tools that extend the body's capabilities — it far exceeded the voice's physical limits. It could produce its tones faster, louder, higher, lower, and longer than any human singer. Despite its ability to suggest consonants and vowels, it could not, of course, talk. But it could do better: it could communicate feeling unburdened by the limitations and perplexities of words.

Opera and violin music, then, naturally grew up together. The great innovator among late Renaissance composers, the Italian Claudio Monteverdi, was both a singer and a violinist, and at the beginning of the seventeenth century he brought the violin family into the orchestras that accompanied his operas — a form that he was busy inventing. In the Baroque century, roughly from 1650 to 1750, solo singers and solo violinists sang similar florid, high-arching melodies. The bowed string was copying the voice, but the voice was also copying the bowed string. Composers of operas and oratorios often used words not as devices for verbal communication but as media for conveying melodies. No one expected to understand what the soprano was saying with her improbably drawn-out vowels and her trills. She was competing with the violin. For stylish singing, and for the expression of emotion through music, words merely got in the way.

After 1760, when Haydn set out to create music that would imitate refined conversation among friends, the choice of the violin family, among the musical technologies available to him, must have seemed inevitable. The string quartet would stand in for four human voices, and with it, free of the shackles of language, he could say whatever he wanted.

A Romantic History

Throughout the history of the string quartet, the alliance between the expressiveness of the bowed string and the expressiveness of the human voice has always remained close. Composers often have the alliance in mind, even if they keep their thoughts about it private; performers discuss it and exploit it; listeners respond to it, even if they aren't aware of it. Beethoven, for example, was not averse to confessing that he expressed emotion in his instrumental compositions in a manner similar to speech. His great nineteenth-century biographer, Alexander

Wheelock Thayer, relates this anecdote concerning the composer's second quartet, published as Opus 18, No. 1:

> The following anecdote ... was told by Beethoven's friend Karl Amenda: After Beethoven had composed his well-known String Quartet in F Major, he played for his friend [Amenda] [on the pianoforte?] the glorious Adagio [D minor, 9/8 time] and asked him what thought had been awakened by it. 'It pictured for me the parting of two lovers,' was the answer. 'Good!' remarked Beethoven, 'I thought of the scene in the burial vault in *Romeo and Juliet*.'"[30]

Beethoven made no marking in the score of this quartet to reveal his thought to performers, but elsewhere he was not so reticent. For the slow movement of his fifteenth quartet (Opus 132, in A minor), he entered the subtitle: "Heiliger Dankgesang eines Genesenen an die Gottheit" (A Convalescent's Hymn of Thanks to the Deity). He entitled the last movement of his last quartet (Opus 135, in F major) "Der schwer gefasste Entschluss" (A Difficult Resolution), and offered an explicit translation of the opening theme. The first mournful, angular minor phrase, in octaves in the viola and cello means: "Must it be?" The jaunty, raucous answer in the violins: "It must be! It must be!" His entry at the top of the score reads:

Muss es sein?

Es muss sein!   *Es muss sein!*

Beethoven does not tell us *what* must be. Death? A trip to the dentist? (According to Thayer, Beethoven, who loved practical jokes, wrote the music first as a vocal canon to twit a friend who was unwilling to pay a bill.[31])

Beethoven's comment that he portrayed the parting of two lovers in his Quartet in F Major Quartet returns to my mind as I listen to Ann, Sharon, Joanna, and Pam learning Borodin's Second Quartet. I have been hearing this music as a portrait of two lovers. In every movement, two of the stringed instruments — not always the same ones — seem to be playing the part of two people as they converse. The conversation is not one to be translated into words. Rather, the melodies in Borodin's quartet express feelings as words might express them, if words were able to express feelings as perfectly as music can.

The first movement begins — just as the Notturno of the third movement will — with a cello melody, which is answered by a similar melody in the first violin. As in the third movement, the viola's and second violin's background is a gentle, off-the-beat pulse. The upward-leaping contour of the melody suggests questioning; the accompaniment, longing. To me, the suggestion of a man's and woman's voices is unmistakable. They meet and think of each other with desire.

Throughout the entire piece, the lovers' voices are heard, represented by different instrumental combinations. In the second movement, they are a couple in a waltz. The two violins are the dancing partners, moving closely together in thirds. In the background, the cello suggests their whirling motion, and the viola lays down the harmony. In the third movement, the nightsong, the cello makes his declaration of love, as he descends in his sighing fourths through the full range of the male human voice. As the violin answers him in the soprano range, the viola's baritone countermelody expresses his caress as he listens.

In the second section of the Notturno, the two voices are again violins, exchanging a quickly rising melody that the composer marks "risoluto" — resolved. "They're talking now," as Joanna puts it. Then the cello and first violin resume the opening love song in duet, the violin playing one measure behind the cello so that the staggered melody harmonizes with itself. Finally both themes — the love duet and the resolved conversation — return together, passing back and forth between all four instruments, in gradually briefer, more languid fragments, until they finally rest on a chord marked *perdendosi,* fading away, as if the sated lovers, in the midst of murmuring endearments, sink at last into sleep.

The fourth movement is much different in mood — it is louder, faster, more dissonant. Still, there are always two voices, now restless and both talking at once. One voice is usually twice as hurried as the other. Occasionally they both stop short. Then viola and cello briefly assume a single male voice to confront the joined violins, as if both sides have doubled their strength to shout at each other. Despite its turbulence, however, the underlying mood of the movement is joy.

It is not too much to conclude that the quartet is a portrait of Borodin's own romantic history. The composer wrote the quartet and dedicated it to his wife, Yekaterina Protopopova, in August, 1881, exactly twenty years after he had proposed to her. It was written just after he had returned from a visit to Heidelberg, where the couple had fallen in love in 1861 and had spent their first six months together.[32] Beyond the dedication, Borodin did not hint in words about his intentions. However, his Russian biographer, Serge Dianin, who was in effect the composer's grandson, argues persuasively that the quartet records in music the history of the Borodins' courtship and marriage.[33] The first movement is a reminiscence of the couple's falling in love, the second recalls the elation of their romance, the third celebrates their lovemaking, while the fourth is a humorous record of their later married life, which was chaotic, stormy, and devoted.

Ann: The first movement of the Borodin is full of love. There's a kind of sensuousness about the quartet because of the relationship between the first violin and the cello. It's a very male-female kind of romance that happens, although it can't be sentimentalized.

Sharon: I'd say romance, more than love, for the first movement. It's not true love yet, it's the grand *idea* of wanting to be in love.

Ann: I definitely hear that. It's very caressive, very warm. And then the second movement is full of joy and fun, it's like a bell going off, sparks flying. In the third movement, the Notturno, there's an interweaving around the notes, for example with the viola countermelody, and a caressing quality that the main melody has, and the kind of pillowed sound in the accompaniment, that suggest physical love. There are lots of hints.

Joanna: I also think, considering when it was written, that it's very innocent. It's not blue-collar music, it's definitely aristocratic, with an element of the intellectual. You've definitely got a flavor of the East with Borodin, but it's also very well thought out and very well crafted and very well structured, so that gives me - - I agree with what the two of you are saying, but it also gives me just a tinge of objectivity.[34]

Pam: The aspect of it that I feel is spectacular is that it also seems to be in the tradition of great ballet, because there's such dance to it. Each movement has something that I see, visualizing an emotion.

Communicating

It has long been considered incorrect, among the majority of writers about music, to speculate in this way about the stories that might be hidden in pieces of instrumental music, or about the feelings that are expressed through the sounds. In this view, the music is merely the music. Why add something else to it? But the majority of composers have ignored this purism. Implicit story-telling, as in Beethoven's portrait of Romeo and Juliet, and as in Borodin's portrait of his own marriage, is, to be sure, only one among several strands that weave through the history of Western music. But instrumental music, including quartets, is nevertheless almost always expressive of emotions. Composers place these expressions in deliberate sequence. That does not necessarily mean that the sequence corresponds to a similar progress of emotions in a separate story outside the music. One can certainly listen to Borodin's quartet, for example, without ever thinking that it might be unfolding a specific extra-musical story. But to listen to it without being aware of its amorous emotions is, perhaps, hardly to listen to it at all.

Modernist musical theory considers the expression of emotion to be a sign of shallowness in a composer, and it considers listening for emotional expression to be a sign of ignorance in an audience. But emotional expressivity is music's natural content. Most of the great modernist composers themselves, however fierce their intellectualism, never succeeded in driving emotion out of their own compositions. Anyone who doubts this should listen in sequence to the four published quartets of Arnold Schoenberg, music's quintessential modernist. The four quartets follow, from 1905 to 1936, the Austrian composer's development from late Romanticism to the absolute modernism of atonal serialism. All four are deeply laden with feeling from beginning to end.

Performers, for their part, must always be searching for the emotional content of what they are playing, proper modernist theory notwithstanding. They are not embarrassed by their task of communicating musical meaning. Performers are in the business of making music to be listened to, and most listeners, for their part, have come to the concert hall, or have put a recording on the stereo, in part because they hope they will be touched by the emotions that they hear.

Sharon: What excites me in a performance is the communication. As a quartet member, if I'm turning on even one audience member out of a thousand to a piece of music that I love — if I've reached their heart with it, if I'm the vehicle that goes from Borodin's heart through their eardrums to their heart, if I'm a vehicle for touching one human being out there in the dark, then I'm satisfied.

Joanna: It's a great thing to be able, first of all, to feel the feelings in the music yourself, when you play, because you have to attempt to recreate the feelings in yourself — and second, to share that with a lot of other people.

Pam: That's true, although I want to say that we don't definitely know that Borodin sat down and said, "I want to write something about love." When it comes down to it, we only know as much of what the composer was expressing as we as human beings can respond to it in feeling it ourselves. We look at the score, and there's another human being there trying to communicate. It moves us and we can hear the possibilities. We think he's after something, but we can't quite understand it, and then we're all the more intrigued to go further and further and further and try to grasp it. That's what studying music is for me.

Sharon: As you mature in life, hopefully you become a little more aware of how Borodin or Beethoven or Shostakovich felt. It's not that you want to get inside their lives, but you want to be able to say something emotionally with your instrument. So in performance, you're getting an emotional high or an emotional low, you're feeling either the lows of anger or the highs of ecstasy and love, or whatever it may be. There's always an emotional impact that you're trying to get across. I think that for all of us, that's the number one priority —

Ann: Communicating.

Sharon: We're communicating an emotion, or a character, and each piece or each part has its character, even if it's a superfluous character, or a fun or a happy-go-lucky character.

Ann: That's why, for me, making music is a chance to be a bit like an actor. These notes in front of me take on a character, so when I hear the opening theme on the cello in the Borodin, say, I'm affected by that, and whatever emotion I'm getting from Pam at that moment, maybe a longing, I'm going to try and respond to in some way.

Joanna: What we've been saying makes me think of a performance by Isaac Stern with the San Francisco Symphony, which I heard when I was a student. He was playing three or four concertos in a row. When he got to the Brahms concerto, the tension and the electricity in the room were at such a height that — I was in standing room with some friends, and we practically fell off the balcony. Everyone in the house was so involved that you couldn't have done anything to destroy the concentration of the audience, let alone the performer.

Pam: That's one reason why I go to performances myself. You're in a room with a lot of other people experiencing the same thing, experiencing the goose bumps. That's what we're all looking for, the goose bumps in life.

One of the chief reasons that quartets are so popular is that stringed instruments lend themselves so readily to direct emotional expression. The overt emotionality of quartets appeals to all the participants in music — composers, performers, and listeners. In particular, the quartet's small size and the similarity of its voices, by imitating the family and the group of friends, invites the expression of feelings that are personal and intimate. In life, we confess our private feelings to spouses, relatives, and friends, not to large groups of people, even if none of them are strangers. Thus in music, composers have long chosen quartets for the working out of private struggles and the recording of inward stories. The grand gestures of an oratorio or a symphony have much less often seemed the right choice to portray the parting of lovers or the story of a marriage. The bareness and simplicity that can be achieved in the quartet sound has recommended it, too, as a medium for meditations on death. A remarkable number of composers, including Beethoven, Schubert, Mendelssohn, Franck, Smetana, Fauré, Janácek, Bartók, Britten, and Shostakovich, have turned to the quartet during the last year or two of their lives.

Music conceals at the same time that it reveals, and that, too, makes the quartet attractive as a confessional. The four quartet instruments, so close to the human voice, nevertheless speak without words, and so composers have been able to proclaim their secret feelings through quartets safely, without suggesting anything specific. Music's lack of specificity is one of the reasons for its universal appeal. Most listeners will agree that, in his last quartet, Shostakovich seems to be mourning his own impending death, yet it is not only his death that we mourn as we listen. Borodin was probably thinking of his wife; still, what emerges from the music is not his love, but anyone's. As the music plays, each performer and listener can respond in sympathy. The music reconnects us with what we already know, through our own lives, about sorrow and terror, about desire, tenderness, and devotion.

II. The Quartet as a Community

1. Subservient Exerters

Waltzing

Pam Highbaugh holds her cello and bow out to her right side. "The second theme," she says, "at measure 29? This is how I hear it moving." She raises her left hand to rest it on the shoulder of an imaginary partner in a waltz. Swaying to the beat, she sings gently another of Alexander Borodin's celebrated melodies:

The melody begins the second section of the second movement of Borodin's quartet. (In the musical comedy *Kismet,* the tune was adapted for the song "Baubles, Bangles, and Beads.") The Lafayette has just played through the movement as it continues its rehearsal, and Pam has sung the tune to begin the critique. "Dee-dah, dee-dah," she sings, tipping her head to look up to her imagined partner as he might be circling her around a ballroom. Then she drops her hand to dispel the dance and slice the air, adding vehemently, "Whereas dee-*dum,* dee-*dum!*" To her ear, the Lafayette has just played the music much too choppily.

Nodding, Sharon lowers her instrument from her collarbone and stands it on her knee. "Yeah. Glitchy."

Almost all the way through the sixty-measure section, the second violin moves in tandem with the first, usually at the interval of a third below the melody — as if the two violins were the waltzers. The section begins:

While the violins move in thirds, on the top two lines of the score, the viola holds down a G to establish the harmony. Meanwhile, the cello's arpeggios, or broken chords, seem to imitate the whirling of the dancers, as Pam has suggested.

To express musical meaning, it is not enough to play the notes in tune and on time. That is only the beginning. The music must have character, must express emotion. The quartet members' decisions concerning the character of Borodin's waltz will determine their choices about musical details. For example, the natural pattern of emphasis in a waltz, with its three beats to a measure, is *one* two three, *one* two three. But Borodin's melody,

with its short-long, short-long pattern, seems to place the emphasis on the second beat — one *two* three, one *two* three. Pam's critique is that the violins have succumbed to this one-*two*-three emphasis. They were creating a thumping waltz instead of a lilting one.

Joanna rests her viola on her lap. "You know," she says,

softening her proposal with politely tentative tags, "I think, I feel like the two parts here are intertwined better if you can feel the downbeat stronger and play off of that." She's agreeing with Pam: it should be *one* two three.

Pam offers: "Would it help if I just tried it with Ann first?"

Reducing the four parts to duets is standard quartet strategy for isolating a problem. Ann, the last to speak in this critique, now says, "Let's try it."

The cello and first violin began the waltz without the others.

Joanna interrupts after the first four bars. "Can you try it again? Pam, your sound-making, I think your sound-making is—"

Pam: "A little heavy, I know, but I'm just trying to—" For the time being, she wants to firmly mark the downbeat, even at the expense of delicacy.

Ann nods and they begin again, then halt after several bars because they aren't in time together, then play through to the end of the waltz. Their new emphasis on the downbeat has not solved the problem. The quartet is still playing the four-measure phrase choppily, with four distinct pulses. *One* two three thumps no less that one *two* three. Ann says: "We're doing it too" — she claps on each *one,* each downbeat — "too One. Two. Three. Four."

Pam nods. "Mm. Right. There's a way for us to interlock, then, because I feel that same thing. I want to play my part so that" — she plays her broken chords without either emphasis. Instead, her whirling notes follow a single arc of growing and lessening volume, so that they reach their loudest moment in the third measure, where both the melody and the accompaniment reach their highest notes. Afterward, in the fourth measure, she lets her sound subside.

Here is her accompanying line, with crescendo and decrescendo markings to indicate increase and decrease in volume.

Now everyone is talking at once. Pam has stated the solution, and at the same time has raised a new question. To avoid the choppiness, the four measures of the melody should be sung in one phrase, should be played as a single circling of the imagined dancers. Perhaps the easiest way to shape a passage of music into a single phrase is to approach and then retreat from a peak in volume. But where in the music should that peak be reached? What shape should be drawn in the sound? Pam's demonstration of the peak at the third measure suggested one shape, but there could be others, and each would suggest a waltz of a different character.

Ann's voice gains over the others'. "But could it be, you see, but that's the exact opposite of what" — and she plays the melody the way she herself hears it. For her, the phrase follows a different curve than it does for Pam: she feels the height of volume and tension should be reached in the second measure, not in the third, even though the third contains the highest note of the melody.

"The first two bars are more full, more sensual," Ann says. She amends Pam's image of the gently swaying waltzers. "He's flung her out in the first two bars, and she's flinging back into him now in the third. She's not breaking loose."

"Right," Pam says, not to agree, but to soften her dissent. "But you know, I don't think you're going to want" — she plays her broken chords to comply with Ann's hearing of the melody, with the peak of volume in the second bar — to her, the wrong way.

"A little bit like that, yes," Ann says. "I do want it a little bit like that."

Pam shakes her head. "I don't. I don't like it that way."

Ann pushes ahead: "Instead of"—and she plays her melody Pam's way. "The thing that I'm feeling is, we're doing too much, to me anyway, I feel like we're still getting too much" — she sings the four-measure phrase ta-*dum,* ta-*dum,* exaggerating the thump that none of them wants. To Ann's ear, peaking the melody in the third measure may be perpetuating the problem, because aiming for the third measure conveys too much tension.

Now the two musicians sing the phrase back and forth to each other, half in open debate, half in search of consensus. The contrast between their competing song-fragments begins to close.

Joanna interrupts, saying dryly, "Well, let's try it."

Cello and first violin again play the entire waltz, more Ann's way than Pam's. At the end, Pam smiles slightly. "Better." She's conceding. She adds, "My feeling is that the more clear it is in terms of phrasing, the better, so whatever you choose to do, Ann"—

Joanna interposes: "Yeah."

Pam continues: "I mean I want to play it in the way that you feel you're observing the line. I want that."

"Right," Sharon says. "Okay." For now, at least, the agreement is sealed.

Deciding

A soloist doesn't have to explain or defend her interpretation of a passage of music. She merely plays it, and if her playing communicates to her listeners her understanding of the music's moods and her sense of its phrases, there is nothing more to be said. As for an orchestral player, she too has no need for speech. Her job is to play as directed. But players of chamber music, if they are to fulfill their obligation to be active members of a musical team, must be able to say what they mean as well as play it. They have to be fluent in metaphors that can translate musical statements and effects into inevitably unsatisfactory equivalents in gestures and words, as Pam translated Borodin's melody into the pantomime of a waltz.

Pam and her colleagues have learned how to identify subtle musical problems and to patiently demonstrate solutions, whether by playing alternatives, by singing, or by offering extra-musical translations. But musicians do not take great pleasure in the labor of consulting and restating. The effort required has discouraged many a string-player from a career in chamber music. Even successful chamber players find words intractable and tedious, at least when the subject under discussion is music. To them, speech is an inferior means of communication, much less subtle than music and much less exact. They would much rather play a piece than talk about it.

> People usually complain that music is so ambiguous, that it leaves them in such doubt as to what they are supposed to think, whereas words can be understood by everyone. But to me it seems exactly the opposite.[35]

So wrote Felix Mendelssohn, who was no doubt speaking for all musicians of every time and place.

> Sharon: Sometimes it's so hard to say what we're doing. Sometimes I feel the more we say words, the more we get tangled up. You suggest something to a colleague and she plays according to what you've said, and it's not what you wanted at all. You say, "No, that's not what I meant." Often you both want the same exact turn of the phrase, but as soon as you say words, it feels like it's become the opposite, or at least it's a shade different in meaning. Finally you just throw up your hands and say—
>
> Ann: You say, "Well, we know what we want."
>
> Sharon: "Don't play what I say, play what I want."

67

Pam: The most gratifying rehearsals are the ones without a lot of speaking. We just keep going at the music, just playing more and more and letting it change. We progress towards that as we get to know a piece.

Ann: If I'm frustrated by something that's been happening in the music, I will try to show it instead of say it. I'll just say, "Can we try that again?" and then I'll do something different with how I'm playing it, rather than saying, "Could we phrase it this way?" I will play it in such a way that I will hope my colleagues will hear. Very often the first violin has the line that is going to dictate the sound of the quartet, essentially, but I don't want to impose my ideas on my colleagues with words. I don't way to say, "I want you to sound like this and you to sound like that," and I easily could, because when I'm playing, I have so many ideas. But I want them to be searching, and they are — always searching for different ways of playing their parts. Of course, if there's something that's just not working with my part, and I find I'm just having to struggle to do it the way I'm trying to do it, then I will say something. Generally, though, I'm going to try and phrase things in a way that they'll hear it, and each will respond in her own way, instinctively respond to it, rather than just consciously. And it usually works.

In the discussion of Borodin's waltz, adequate translations emerged. Agreement about the shape of the waltz phrase was soon reached — but only because Pam yielded. She gave way for several reasons. In the first place, enough time had been spent on the discussion, and this was only the first of many rehearsals of the movement. Everyone knew that the agreement to play the waltz Ann's way, with the peak on the second measure, was subject to later evolution. All musicians agree that there is no one right way to interpret a piece of music — although there are certainly wrong ways. The stereotype of the mercurial musician is not without basis: music is not a profession for the mind that prefers certainty. And in fact, by the time the Lafayette recorded Borodin's quartet, seven months later, they were not reaching a peak in that debated phrase at all — neither in the third measure nor the fourth — but instead much later on in the waltz, which by then had become a single seamless sixty-measure melody.[36]

Pam yielded, too, because Ann was after all playing the melody, and the melodist must usually be granted the last word in a competition between two equally convincing interpretations. Thus Pam said to Ann, to close the discussion: "I want to play it in the way that you feel you're observing the line." After the rehearsal, she added in explanation:

Sometimes I feel really strongly how a passage should go, and maybe what I'm hearing is not exactly what I want. But if I hear something convincing coming back, I want to play into it. When I'm not happy is when I don't hear anything to play into.

In choosing between possible interpretations, the quartet was not seeking for compromise. They didn't want an amicable middle ground, with each member settling for some of what she wanted but not all, in the manner appropriate to the checks and balances of public life. In art, compromise invites the danger of mediocrity.

Joanna: When we have different ideas about how things go, sometimes what happens is that during the process, we'll argue and argue and then we'll whittle the ideas down so that they're not those ideas any more but only halfway those ideas. And that's not the best way to do things. I would rather see a strong idea and a strong idea and try them both and then make a decision for one or the other. That's musically more interesting than to try to get a homogenized version of something. So when we choose, it's better for one person to give in. We each know we're going to get our chance another time. But we all have to be flexible and let each other have their say first, because we all have a stake in it.

Balancing

Thus the very nature of quartet music — the blending of four similar, soloistic voices that continually take turns standing in the limelight of the melody and then retreating to the shadows of accompaniment — is recapitulated in the social organization of the four musicians who play. The paradigm of teamwork embodied in quartet music becomes realized in the actual professional relations of the living players. When the four are at work together in rehearsal, whether or not their bows are on the strings, they need to know when to take the lead — as Ann did in critiquing the accompanying chords at the opening of the third movement of the Borodin, and as Sharon did in the discussion of the viola countermelody which follows — and when to get out of the way, as Pam did in the critique of the waltz. They also need to know how to mediate — a role Joanna often takes, just as her viola mediates between the upper and lower registers in the music. They must listen as attentively during verbal critique as they do when they are playing. In their work together, then, all four need to achieve a balance between forceful assertion and graceful collegiality, between their individual creativity and their loyalty to the goals of the group. When all can maintain this balance, teamwork can thrive.

Joanna: If we were all little girls on the playground in the fifth grade, we would be the ones who would be telling the other kids we were playing with what they should do. "Okay, now you're going to be this, and you're going to do that." All of us in the quartet would be that. We wouldn't be followers. So in our quartet, and in any quartet if it's going to be a good one, in my opinion, you're going to have four leaders. And that's when we get into big trouble, personality trouble with each other. Whenever you have to make a decision, it can be hard, because no one wants to be told how to think, no one wants to be told what they want. That's true when we have to make business decisions, and it's the same thing when we're working on the music. I want it this way, and someone else says, "No, that won't work." That makes you say, "Oh, yes it will" even more. So you have to know when to give it up.

Ann: If we all didn't have rather enlarged egos, we wouldn't be in this business. We would all be playing in an orchestra and feeling somewhat happy doing that. I don't know anybody in this quartet who has a small ego. Nobody. And I think that goes along with any quartet situation. The idea is that ego is being nurtured and held at bay, nurtured and held at bay, so that there's a growing, so that each one of us in the quartet does become stronger and more convincing, and so that all of the good qualities that ego produces happen when we make music. When you listen to the Alban Berg Quartet, who we studied with, you don't hear a lack of ego there. You hear an incredibly — I don't want to say "virile," because that's putting a sexist word on it, but you hear very convinced men there in the music. And any great quartet achieves that fine balance between the ego and the group. That what makes it *so* hard, and that's why so many soloists would never make it in a quartet, because they only need the nurturing, they can't tolerate the checking.

Joanna: For the kind of ego you need to be a soloist or a conductor, you need the strokes.

Ann: They also need to have correcting, but they won't accept it. In quartet, you need to be an exerter, but a subservient exerter.

Joanna: Yes! That's great!

Pam: The only question I would have about what you've said, is whether it is always ego. Or is it an assurance, a confidence about what you're doing, that allows you more inner working, more change, more flexibility? I wonder if the ego part isn't too helpful in making four voices work together. I would say that quartet may not always feed the right things for people, and it's not for everyone at every stage of their life, I think. I would be the first to say that there are days when I'm not sure it's where I want to be at the time. But it's also a fire that refines. I think work does that for everyone; it's the nature of work. You are having to work with other people, and no man is an island. But when you make music in a quartet, you're having to put your passion and some of your deepest feelings forward in a vehicle with other people, and what you produce is going to be identified not just with yourself but with a combination of all of you. To make the music you need to have your individualism, and it's something you have to kind of fight for, but also give up.

Joanna: Every day is different, depending on how everybody feels. I think my personality is more objective than the others', and if somebody's got a really strong bent one way or the other, a lot of times I will stay out of it. I'll let it go, because there are very strong personalities in the group, and what I've found over the years is that you can keep asserting yourself and asserting yourself and then you find that you're just battling egos rather than making the music happen. So I'll set something I want aside and just go along, and if it ends up not working for me, or if it's something I feel really strongly about, I'll try to find the best time to speak up about it, which may not always be right away. I don't just blurt out everything I'm thinking, and sometimes I get criticized for being too objective in quartet. But if somebody is making a lot of comments one day and saying how things should go and trying their ideas and is really into it, I don't feel uncomfortable about just letting her do that, even if that means that my ideas aren't going to be out there in the forefront. Because you can't force your point of view on the others. You simply can't do that. It's better to give and take. You have to be willing to give somebody else's idea a chance and do it wholeheartedly. I find that for me — although it doesn't always work — I want to look at it this way: if I give that to my colleagues, they're going to give it back.

The competitive turn-taking necessary to rehearsal takes on a different tenor in performance. When the quartet is on stage, give-and-take is superseded by empathy.

Ann: We've been together now for a long time. Each of us knows now: I can depend on these people. I can take off and just land. Pam can take off on those glisses in Murray Schafer's first quartet, which we'll be performing in Europe this fall — *dooooo, yah!* — and we know we're not going to beat her to that top note, because we're sensing. We're sensing. She's high. She's going for it. There's something happening over there, so be aware. — And we each do that for each other in a performance situation. It's teamwork. There's none of that feeling we can have in rehearsal of, "Well, *I* don't think *this* should go *this* way. I would certainly want to change *that.*" Instead, it's: "What is she doing? What is she doing there?"

Sharon: I'm rubbing up against the other three parts, and then suddenly I have a little one-or-two-measure second-violin solo, a little *moment musicale,* and if I come out so intently at the beginning of it that my colleagues can't help listening to me, then if I want to do something extra, then boom, they'll be there with me.

Pam: With a lot of spur-of-the-moment expressive things like that, we don't even talk to each other about them in advance, because they're just a matter of voicing. At the moment of playing it's, "Why don't I use more bow on this note?"

Ann: Probably ninety-five percent of the time, you don't even have a conscious thought about it before you do it.

Pam: And then when you hear your colleague play in a certain way, you'll adjust your intonation to fit hers, for example, or your articulation. Especially in a piece from the Classical period, if it's a fugue or some other kind of conversational thing, and someone starts it off by playing it longer than you expected, you're onto the moment — that's the fun of it — and you play the thing back to her her way. We try to inspire each other by playing it in a little different manner.

Ann: When you get up on stage, it's the ultimate moment of truth, and I have to trust these three women with everything I'm doing. I have to trust that they're going to be listening. It's like a team at the highest level of basketball: when you throw the ball, you're not even looking, but you know that your teammate is going to be there. That kind of feeling is there on stage for all of us, and that is the really wonderful thing.

Quartet performers and listeners often make the comparison, as Ann did, between the tossing of a melody among the players and the tossing of a ball down a basketball court, or across a baseball infield. One of the delights of attending a live quartet performance, especially in a small hall, is that one can see the teamwork between the players as well as hear it between the musical lines. As in sports, so in chamber music, and so in work and in the family: people act in concert, taking the risk of trusting one another. This must always be part of the meaning of quartet music, in whatever style it was composed, in whatever century.

Staying Married

It is no wonder that sociologists who investigate the dynamics of small groups sometimes study string quartets as quintessential work communities.[37] Quartet players are perhaps more intensely dependent on one another than are members of any other kind of team, except the family.[38] Interdependence among quartet members reached its greatest compression in earlier generations. The British cellist Colin Hampton has recalled, for example, that before he and his colleagues of the Griller Quartet emigrated to the United States in 1949, they played over 250 concerts a year together and rehearsed ten to twelve hours a day, six days a week. After the quartet was formed in 1928, the four members set up joint housekeeping, and after the marriage of Sidney Griller, the first violinist and leader, in 1932, the second violinist and the violist continued to live with him for eleven more years.[39]

Among quartets nowadays, such domestic devotion, such incessant rehearsal, and such relentless concertizing are all considered not only unnecessary but dangerous to the quartet's survival. In North America, where audiences are fewer and concert halls farther apart than in Europe, most quartets play no more than a hundred concerts a year, and they limit rehearsals to three or four hours, five days a week, to allow time for teaching. Still, regular rehearsals cannot be avoided, and touring still throws the players together, away from their families, for weeks at a time. Many quartets attempt to mitigate their mutual exposure by avoiding each other outside of work hours and by making separate travel arrangements on tour. They may deliberately fly on different airlines and stay in different hotels. Nevertheless, quartet players often compare their professional association to a marriage.

Ann: We've often used that analogy. We really do feel married to each other.

Sharon: When my husband Mark Franklin and I first talked about marriage, he already knew that he would be marrying Sharon Stanis and he would be marrying the life of the Lafayette Quartet. He was well aware of that. He's aware that five years, ten years from now I may come to him and say, 'Mark, the quartet wants to move to — say, Georgia. There's the dreamiest residency in the world in such-and-such university in Georgia. What are we going to do?' Obviously he and I still have the right to say no. I have the right to leave the quartet. But he knows the kind of pressure that could be upon us.

In 1991, when the Lafayette left its first base in Detroit to assume its position at the University of Victoria, Ann was the only married member. Her husband, Robert Goldschmid, gave up his Michigan law practice and followed his wife to Canada, where he undertook a year and a half of training and apprenticeship to meet the requirements of the British Columbia bar. Pam's husband, Yariv Aloni, a violist, left his own quartet and university position to join Pam in Victoria upon their marriage in 1994. (Sharon met Mark Franklin in Victoria, where he was already established as an independent digital audio engineer. Joanna is single.) Of course, were the members of the Lafayette all male, the willingness of their spouses to relocate would be nothing remarkable. The professional flexibility of Ann's and Pam's husbands bespeaks the gains made in their generation towards the righting of the balance of power between the genders. But it is evidence, also, of the power in the commitment that drives the Lafayette forward.

Sharon: We always said that — since for several years Ann was the only married one, and we knew she wanted to have a child — we always said, "Ann, we don't want to put pressure on you." — "Oh, don't worry. When Bob and I decide to have a child, we'll come and ask you guys." — Not that she was going to ask our permission. She'll do what she wants. But she also wanted to consult us, because obviously her having the baby was going to affect our rehearsal schedule, our concert schedule, our recording schedule. Our lives are so interconnected that we have to respect how the other people will be influenced.

All-male quartets have not had to face this dilemma. A member and his wife decide to have a child, his wife has the child, his quartet cancels one or two concerts, he shows up at the delivery room, and then a day or two later he's on the road with his colleagues, playing the next concert. Obviously that can't work for us. There's no precedent for what we're doing. We're trailblazers for this. Yes, there are some quartets with women in them that are making it work with children, but usually two or three of the members are male.

For many quartet players, the intensity of their dependence upon their colleagues is sometimes beyond bearing. A professional commitment that sometimes feels like a marriage often becomes such a demanding rival to real family life that one or the other must be abandoned. Even when families are not threatened, many players find they cannot endure the unrelenting propinquity of their colleagues, especially when on tour. In the daily grind of rehearsals, too, resentment and dispute are inevitable.

String players blunder into the challenge of getting along with each other when they first enroll in a student quartet in conservatory. Every teacher of chamber music occasionally finds herself a group therapist guiding fractious student egos through petty disputes so that their quartet can finish out the semester. Among professional ensembles, the wearing task of intense collaboration year in and year out becomes one of the two main causes of dissolution. (The other is economic hardship.) Quartets often continue as teams for several decades, but there is almost always turnover among individual members. To continue together even for ten years without a single change in personnel, as the Lafayette has done, is already unusual. The Amadeus Quartet, the great post-war British ensemble, remained intact for forty years; the four Americans of the Guarneri Quartet have continued together since 1964; but they are exceptions. Such longevity has always been rare.

Some quartets have become celebrated for their disputatiousness — for example, the great Russian-American ensemble, the Budapest Quartet. The hallmark of the Budapest's performances was an expressive informality. The quartet's playing was so informal, in fact, that on their recordings the four musicians are not always in agreement about when to begin a phrase, and they occasionally seem to be disagreeing about who has the melody as they struggle to push each other out of the spotlight. The spontaneity and occasional contentiousness of their performances mirrored their professional relationships as colleagues. Their rehearsals were notoriously long-winded, acrimonious, and disordered. They were said to dislike, even to hate each other — although their biographer, Nat Brandt, argues persuasively that the acrimony masked a mutual devotion.[40]

The Budapest's famous students, the members of the Guarneri Quartet, have likewise made no apology for their own well-known disputes. When a 1991 documentary video chronicled the Guarneri's contentious rehearsals, an interviewer who was also a fan complained about the unflattering video footage. David Soyer, the group's cellist, replied:

> What did you expect to see us do in rehearsal? Agree? Then we would have nothing to say. It's in the nature of rehearsals to be negative. We don't say: "That was very good, let's do it that way;" — it's always, "No, let's not do it that way."[41]

Chronic battling in rehearsal leads members of not a few quartets to become thoroughly sick of one another. They mask their mutual distaste in public, and they may well succeed in countering their resentments for years with their shared love of the music and with the intense cooperation needed for playing quartets in performance. Members of lesser fortitude resign from such quartets. In the words of the violist of an American quartet that has replaced its second violinist once and its first violinist twice in its fifteen years:

> The public doesn't know how much goes into this work. Interpersonally, it's grueling. You spend so much time with people who may not be the ones you'd necessarily chose to spend time with otherwise. A lot of time gets used deconstructing why you said what you said — digging through the feces. You have to, if you're going to maintain the quartet. People who invite us out together socially, after a concert for example, don't realize we don't want to socialize together — although hopefully we bring it off with grace.[42]

Like every quartet, the Lafayette has had to find a way to live with mutual dependency and inevitable contention.

> Ann: People look at a lot of quartets and they'll say, "My, they're remarkably nice to each other." But there are always hidden things, and in the initial stages of the Lafayette Quartet, a lot of the communication skills that we were developing were not good, necessarily, and had to be unlearned as time went on and we matured. For example, in my New Brunswick background — boy, you just didn't discuss things, you just didn't argue, or if you did argue, it was generally not highly communicative. And then getting in a group with some-

one like Sharon — all her family does is talk to each other constantly. She really has to raise her voice in her family for it to be heard over somebody else's. So when she'd come back from being at home, it would be, "Shhhhh, Sharon."

Sharon: In my family, you erupt. You say exactly what's on your mind, you explode, and as soon as you're done, then it's fine. It's over, no hard feelings. Obviously this needed adjusting when I got into a quartet. Now I don't erupt as primitively, maybe, as I used to. There are still vestiges of those eruptions, but they're in a little different manner, a little more tempered.

Ann: Whereas in my family it wasn't quite like that. We're a little more English, a little more subdued. So I had a hard time with confrontation when we started in quartet. I would often just get paranoid, I would find myself leaving the room, because I couldn't handle differences of opinion that were so strong. I've really changed, a lot. We all have. I've learned to take criticism and accept it and give it.

Joanna: At first it drove me crazy, because I didn't have an effective way of dealing with it. It was sometimes very bad at the beginning, and I couldn't step back and not take it personally. At conservatory, I played in a quartet with two violinists who were already at a professional level. The second violinist would say to the first violinist, "You know, that sounds really terrible. Play that off the string" — spiccato. So she'd shrug and play it off the string and go, "I don't know, I liked it the other way." And they'd be totally congenial about the whole thing. But I could see that if someone had said that to me like that, I would have said, "Screw you, I'm not going to play it off the string."

Sharon: Sometimes we still make some very strong statements for or against. You don't mean to hurt anyone personally, but you have to air your feeling.

Joanna: Because if we want to be honest in our relationships with each other, we have to be willing to get out the bad stuff. If I'm holding something against Sharon or Ann or Pam, I want to have the freedom to bring it up, and then we can duke it out and get it over with, so that we can keep going in the quartet.

Sharon: If there's something stirring, then there's someone who's going to say it. Even if it's eruptive, that's better than burying it.

Ann: One of us will do it.

Sharon: We'll say, "This really pisses me off. Now what the hell are you trying to do?" And just go for it. And in a lot of ways, I really would rather have it resolved than buried over.

Joanna: I think the difference between our quartet and a lot of others could come from the difference between a relationship among women and a relationship among men. I find in my own experience with all-male quartets, and what I've read and heard about, is that a lot of them don't duke it out.

Sharon: They like to bury it.

Joanna: That's probably a factor. But I want to add that a fight amongst all of us can actually affect the way we rehearse or we perform in a very positive way. I don't think there are too many jobs where you can sit down with somebody and say, "This is how I see it, and you're not ..., or you need to ...," and you can have a serious, maybe unpleasant confrontation, and then have that come to a positive end, and then keep growing from that and keep going.

It's not only fighting, though. In our job, we're our own boss, and we can sit in rehearsal and bring out every aspect of our lives there. We don't have to act a certain way or put on a professional image. I've had straight jobs where you couldn't be silly, you couldn't be loud, you couldn't be as creative, you couldn't experiment and have something not work and say, "Okay, scratch that, try something else." I feel that the mixture of these four people in this group makes it possible for me, and I hope for my colleagues, to be all the aspects that we are, so that we can bring more to the music, because we're all exploring every aspect, and I don't think there are very many jobs where you get paid and make a living that you can do that.

For quartets to survive, members must either learn to bury their grievances or, like the Lafayette, to work through their disputes openly in order to reach consensus. Otherwise, weak or unhappy members will quit or be forced out, and if they cannot be replaced, the entire ensemble will founder. Dissolution is most likely in the group's early years, when money is likely to be scarce. Even suicide as an outcome is not unknown. The Griller Quartet, which was the leading British quartet of the generation previous to the Amadeus, ended in 1961 with the suicide of its violist, Philip Burton. The Budapest Quartet continued despite the suicide in 1955 of Jac Gorodetzky, one of the two second violinists who replaced Alexander Schneider during his ten-year absence from the group.

2. Leaders and Democrats

First Fiddle

A s they learn to manage their intense interdependence in order to survive, quartets must resolve a special conundrum: the role of the first violinist. In the music, the first violin is the natural leader. As the highest voice, it is the easiest to hear and the obvious choice for the melody. But if a quartet is to be a quartet and not a violin solo with a backup string band, the first violin's power must be distributed among the other players. This was the paradox that Josef Haydn undertook to solve in the 1770's, and it must still be solved each time a composer sits down to write a quartet. The same problem presents itself every time a group of players comes together to perform quartets. The first violinist plays what is usually the lead voice. Does that mean that he or she is to be the leader of the group?

In the eighteenth century, before the quartet was invented, successful violinists were soloists in concertos and, when they played chamber music, lead players in trio sonatas, which treated the first violinist as a soloist. But Haydn's experiments with the quartet deliberately began to diminish the dominance of the first violin, and by the 1820's, Beethoven and Schubert were writing quartets that treated the four voices almost equally. Performing first violinists of the time, however, were not about to surrender their traditional superiority in deference to radical ideas of musical equality promulgated by composers. In this new chamber music of quartets, they were determined to remain the leaders, as they had always been. Beethoven made it clear that he had little use for the egos of violin virtuosos, but his was a minority view.

Throughout the nineteenth century, flamboyant showmen on the violin and on the piano dominated the musical stage. Quartets were often founded by violin soloists, who without question took the position of first violinist. They often named the new ensembles after themselves, and they usually acted as musical and social dictators. Some stood in performance while their colleagues stayed put in their chairs.[43] One result was to diminish the status of the second violinist. Thus arose the demeaning idiom, "to play second fiddle." What the second violinist lacked was not musical importance, but social power within his professional team.

Joseph Joachim — to use as an example the most eminent first violinist of his generation — was, first and foremost, a virtuoso soloist. He established the Joachim Quartet in 1869 as a performing sideline. A classicist among Romantics, as was his friend Johannes Brahms, Joachim championed the quartets of Beethoven, Mendelssohn, Brahms, and Dvorák. As a soloist in sonatas and concertos, he disdained to make a display of his technique with the shallow prestidigital showpieces that were the common currency of nineteenth-century concert halls. Nevertheless, he ruled his quartet as master. No mere cellist would have dared question his interpretation of a melody in a Brahms quartet as Pam questioned Ann's reading of Borodin's waltz. To Joachim, Brahms himself deferred. Two cellists, three violists, and four second violinists served in turn under Joachim, but when the master died in 1907, the quartet disbanded.

In championing the string quartet, Joachim was opposing the prevailing taste of his age. Most composers, performers, and audiences considered quartets to be an esoteric form. But it has to be said the performers were partly to blame. First violinists who presented themselves as overbearing soloists in string quartets, as they stood beside their seated colleagues, were missing the point of the music they were playing. They were thwarting the quartet's fundamentally communal purpose. Their audiences could not have been hearing what the composers had intended. That may well be one reason why quartets lost much of their popularity during the nineteenth century.

First Among Equals

The dictatorial rule of the first violinist was gradually relaxed among quartets formed in Europe after the First World War. These quartets, joining in the revival of chamber music that was led by composers, understood that collegiality must be the basis of quartet playing. Where and when to perform, what repertory to offer, what fees to accept, when to rehearse, whom to settle on as replacement of a member who had resigned — some or all of these decisions, depending on the quartet, devolved from the first violinist's prerogative onto the consensus of the whole quartet. On stage, these quartets performed as true teams — often placing the first and second violins across from each other, with the cellist sitting next to the first violin. Even so, the first violinist remained the first among equals and continued to lead the quartet in rehearsals as musical director. As in Joachim's time, the leadership was often acknowledged in the naming of the ensemble. Several of the great European quartets of the 1930's and 1940's — the Kolisch from Austria, the Griller from Britain, the Busch from Germany — carried their first violinist's name. Even now the practice of naming a quartet for its leader has not entirely disappeared.[44]

Today, musical leadership by the first violinist survives in many European and in some North American quartets. In these quartets, it is still the first violinist who sets the paces of rehearsals and who speaks with the final voice in musical matters. It is he or she who rules, after discussion, how a phrase should be turned, how the bows should produce the sound together, how fast the piece should be played, what musical character is to be expressed. However, granting the leadership to the first violinist no longer means that the first violin part will be overemphasized in performance. Rather, appointing a leader is a strategy for resolving disputes and for ensuring efficient rehearsals.

A typical first violinist's musical directorship has been described by the late Rostislav Dubinsky, who was a founder and for thirty years the first violinist and leader of the Borodin String Quartet, Russia's most distinguished post-war ensemble.

I believe very deeply that the first violinist should naturally be a conductor. He has to know the piece before he comes to the first rehearsal, and his score should be marked in detail, not only bowings, according to his ideas and understanding, but even sometimes fingerings. Of course there will be discussions and arguments, but not at the first stage.

At the beginning, when we started the Borodin Quartet in 1946 as students at the Moscow Conservatory, we worked in darkness. We knew very little about quartets. We just played, and occasionally someone would say something. As we started to work more deeply, there were arguments, and we decided that each one of us would be director of a certain piece. One person would be responsible for bringing this piece to concert level. And that was the beginning of the idea of having a musical director in the quartet.

Later, during the last ten or twelve years before I emigrated to the West [in 1976], it was just agreed between us that someone would be responsible for the rehearsal, to prepare the quartet for performance, to make the pieces ready. It was my job as first violinist to think and prepare, and the others would work with my idea and comment and maybe disagree, but basically accept the musical leadership. And those were the happiest years.

In Dubinsky's view, vesting the leadership in the first violinist also promotes musical excellence, simply because one player has been given the freedom to interpret the music boldly. When musical decisions are reached through democratic consensus, boldness sometimes gives way to mediocrity.

What I have seen in many American quartets is that the democratic approach doesn't lead to the best results, at least until they find each other. The most common thing is: "Okay, okay. Let's check the metronome, what the composer wrote. Let's just play it according to his tempi." More or less it gets settled, but it never leads to a deep and personal performance.[45]

String Quartet Democracy

It was another Russian quartet, the Budapest, that made the first decisive step toward a new model of quartet governance. The Budapest was founded in 1917 by three Hungarians and a Dutchman who were fellow students at the Budapest Academy of Music. According to the quartet's biographer, the founding first violinist, Emil Hauser, younger than his colleagues and also shyer, had neither the authority nor the inclination to rule over his colleagues. The four friends resolved to decide everything — both musical and business matters alike — by vote. Josef Roismann, the first of the four Russian exiles who eventually replaced all the quartet's founders, joined in 1927 as second violinist and later replaced Hauser as first. But he too disliked ruling and refused to assume a leader's role. The quartet's most flamboyant personality, though not its leader, was the violinist who replaced Roismann on second — Alexander Schneider.[46]

In 1938, the members of the Budapest, now all Russian despite the group's name, emigrated to the United States. There, by its example and through its many students, the ensemble established what became an American style of democratic quartet organization. Two generations later, most North American quartets are leaderless, and the pattern has spread among younger European quartets as well. The Lafayette has been a democracy from the start.

In such quartets, nothing important, musical or otherwise, is decided without agreement by all four members. Onerous business tasks are delegated: thus in the Lafayette, Pam has taken over the bookkeeping from Sharon, Ann makes the travel arrangements, Joanna keeps the library of press clippings and oversees contractual relations with recording executives, and everyone takes turn giving interviews with the press.

Ann: In a quartet, you can't have a prima donna. Unless it's set out at the beginning that the first violinist is going to be the dominant force, and everyone respects that, it's not going to work. The first violinist is the leader in some quartets, and every first violinist in the world would love to have that situation probably, but in American quartets it really hasn't worked out. Quartets have broken up over it. It just isn't how relationships can work here.

Sharon: This quartet is a democracy. I don't think my being second violinist has any bearing on how we make decisions. We're all equal and we all try to make that happen.

Pam: I would go further and say that a string quartet is one of the most democratic societies that you *could* have, if not *the* most.

Pros and Cons

How much leadership, if any, the first violinist is to exercise must be clearly decided upon before a quartet can begin to flourish as an ensemble. But neither method of organization, democracy or first-violin leadership, can ensure peace in rehearsal. As Dubinsky observes, radical equality may lead to gridlock. On the other hand, disputes do not disappear merely because it has been agreed that one member will have the last word. The Amadeus Quartet, for example, was led by its first violinist, Norbert Brainin. The four men were known for a mutual devotion. Upon the death in 1987 of the quartet's violist, Peter Schidlof, the surviving musicians dissolved the quartet rather than replace their colleague. But, as the cellist, Martin Lovett, has recalled,

> We had the most diabolical rows. Any sensitive musician will disagree about whether to play a note short or long, whether you're too flat or too sharp. People have walked out of [our] rehearsals saying, "That's it. I'm never coming back." But we always did.[47]

Brainin kept his leader's chair in the quartet through musical persuasiveness and through his care to let his colleagues vent their views before he ruled. He told an interviewer in 1980:

> There are no compromises in music. If there is a compromise, then somebody's unhappy, and this is the germ of a future disagreement and might lead to the break-up of the group. If you don't argue passionately, you just disintegrate. Of course, the leader has to have the best argument, because if he doesn't, he won't be leader much longer.[48]

But playing in quartet requires unrelenting exposure of one's emotional depth and the open testing of one's skill, and therefore members are easily bruised by an insensitive leading hand.

Dubinsky succeeded in leading the Borodin Quartet not only by his readiness with the best musical argument, to use Brainin's phrase, but by his ability to conduct rehearsals and dispense critiques with great clarity and charm.[49] On the other hand, if a first-violinist leader lacks charm or charisma, if he is too curt or too masterful to succeed as a diplomat, if his decisions are not musically persuasive, then the other members may learn to hate him. A second violinist who survived for twenty-five years in a leading American quartet has recalled:

> You can't get past the first violinist. The lead voice makes choices and you can't ignore them. So leadership from the first violinist is inevitable. In rehearsal and performance, though, the psyches of all four members are on the line. Performance can feel like a public divesting of one's pants. It's the same in rehearsal. You can get so you hate each other's guts. It can be very wearing.[50]

An American sociologist, J. Keith Murnigham, who studied string quartets in Britain in 1981, found a model there that lay halfway between anarchistic American democracy and the older Continental model of strong command by the first violinist. In all but one of the twenty British quartets that Murnigham interviewed, business decisions were shared, but the first violinist made the musical decisions, although he entertained discussion and listened to argument. The other members accepted the first violinist's leadership while maintaining, at the same time, that all four members were equal. In some cases, it was obvious to the observing sociologist that the first violinist was running the rehearsals, but the members themselves were not fully aware of it. One first violinist, Murnigham reported,

> ... responded as if the group was a democracy. ([He said:] "If you're going to get along, ... you have to recognize that you all have feelings about certain things"). But [he] was clearly in charge of rehearsals.... He controlled almost all the stopping and starting.
>
> [Nevertheless] the second violinist of the group said, "I don't think he has any more influence than anyone else," and, "We take turns leading in rehearsal." The cellist agreed: "He doesn't direct the rehearsals."[51]

Murnigham concluded:

Espousing democracy may be the philosophical basis for participative decision-making; at the same time, groups typically need leaders. Having a member fulfill the leadership role while others simultaneously feel that they have an equal say in things effectively satisfies both sides of the leader-democracy paradox.[52]

Perhaps this sort of gracefully adaptive doublethink is peculiar to the British, who can manage to be class-conscious and democratically minded at the same time. In North America — not only in quartets, of course, but in many other walks of life — the danger is neither a Continental dictatorship nor a British muddle but a fractious anarchy.

In quartets governed by the first violinist in the more traditional European manner, it is the second violinist who is the least stable member, the one most likely to resign when professional relationships founder. If they are indeed playing second fiddle, second violinists may be waiting to quit, perhaps in order to form a quartet of their own, in which they will play on first. But in democratic quartets, it is often the first violinists who leave instead, since they are denied that leadership which belongs to the tradition and which is constantly being suggested by their dominance of the melodic line. Players of the lower voices of North American quartets sometimes find themselves recruiting a new first violinist — a situation that is unusual in Europe. Several American quartets — the Guarneri in recent years, for example, and the Emerson since its founding — have partly disarmed the conflict by having the two violinists take turns in the roles of first and second.

Sisters

Despite the disputes that strain the bonds within every quartet, the four members of the Lafayette have been able to persevere together into their thirteenth year. They have learned how to cooperate, in Ann's phrase, as subservient exerters, and how to defuse resentments, as Joanna said, by duking it out. Like most other younger quartets, too, they are steadied and guided toward agreement by their mutual loyalty to a coach and mentor. (The Lafayette's mentor was Rostislav Dubinsky from the quartet's founding until Dubinsky's death in 1997.) Ann, Sharon, Joanna, and Pam are fortunate, also, in having achieved what many quartet players never achieve: an enduring mutual affection that is apart from their respect for one another as professionals. Their personal bond reveals itself in their manner of finishing each other's sentences, as if they were engaged in a rapid exchange of melodies, and in their willingness, as well, to listen without interrupting while one colleague speaks several paragraphs, as if she were playing an extended solo. It is a bond of the nature of their music. Whether it is a bond that in other circumstances would be called friendship, the quartet itself is unable to say.

Pam: Correct me, all of you, if I'm wrong — but I've heard this come out of all of our mouths — I wouldn't say we would consider ourselves close friends. What's binding us to each other is the fact that for more than ten years we've been going through this story, which is an essential part of all of our lives, and a very time-consuming part of our lives, too. When we're on tour, especially, we have no other part of our lives with us, except through the phone. Of course, what we have with each other is something of the nature of friendship, but it's a different glue than what causes people to be close friends. I think because we're not close friends, but colleagues, we can keep the professional relationship. We can expect of each other what we expect, and say to each other the things that we say. That's lucky for us, because I don't think any of us would want to be in a group where that wasn't really embedded in a lot of respect and genuine love for each other, but in a realm that — I spend my life trying to figure out how this is, exactly. But we've really tried to keep that difference.

Sharon: I remember talking to you guys at the beginning and saying I wanted us to be great business partners, great intimate chamber music partners, but not necessarily to be close friends.

Joanna: But you can't deny the three of us know you a lot better than most people do.

Sharon: Exactly. I agree. You know me better than my sisters do.

Pam: Yes, it's true, and people do look at us and think we know about each other completely. But then we were the last to know that Sharon was dating Mark. It was something she kept secret almost until they were engaged. We don't necessarily know each other's personal lives — it's better not to. But it's complicated, because we have to know the inner essence of each other in a way that you don't ever have to in a lot of other work.

Ann: I don't know if this will shed another light on this, but I look at it differently. I take a little issue with what all of you have said. I do consider each one of you my close friends, but *outside* of the quartet. So, if I'm over at Sharon's place, or we're out doing something, going out to dinner or something, quartet is not there.

Pam: Right.

Ann: At that moment it's not a part of the relationship. Each one of us is able to divorce ourselves from the business aspect of our lives.

The Lafayette ignores the common wisdom that the intense propinquity of rehearsal and performance should be tempered with a studied distance outside of work. After more than twelve years together, the four women still respond to the high of a concert with an unwillingness to let each other go. They sometimes need a dinner out together in order to disengage. At home, they'll often attend concerts or make weekend excursions in various ad hoc pairs or trios. "They're like sisters," their friends say. Ann's explanation is, "We like each other."

3. The Sound of Community

Delineation and Blend

The quality of the personal relations among the players in a quartet and the choices they have made about governance are chiefly, but not only, a private concern of the quartet's members. The players' interpersonal balances are inevitably translated into the sound they make together in public performance. Quartet democracy in North America has fostered a style of playing which emphasizes the distinctness of the individual voices over their merging into a single sonority. To the listening ear, the four are more present than the one. Samuel Rhodes — who since 1969 has been the violist of the most celebrated American quartet, the Juilliard — has described this choice:

> The notion many people have that a quartet must be made up of perfectly matched players would make for a dull group indeed. What is necessary is the desire and technique to blend and yet for each to hold and guard jealously his individual way.[53]

Rhodes' view contrasts with the more traditional pursuit of a unified sound. In Rostislav Dubinsky's words:

> The idea in quartet is to bring all instruments to sound like one. That's actually what a string quartet is, one instrument on sixteen strings, and what is more important, one mind.[54]

The deliberate separation of the four string voices results in what has become known as the American sound. An opposite term, the European sound, has been coined in contrast, to name the blended effect described by Dubinsky. The terms are not geographically accurate. Some American quartets have sought as zealously as any European group to create a closely unified sound (the Tokyo and the Cleveland Quartets, for example), while some younger European quartets emulate an individual- istic "American" voicing. Besides, professional players are not pleased to be scolded in reviews for knowing only how to de- lineate the voices, but not to blend them — or vice versa. A quar- tet would rather be heard to move from one effect to the other, according to what is called for by the music. Nevertheless, a real spectrum, along which most quartets do fall, stretches be- tween these stereotypical extremes.

The differences in the sound emerge largely from bowings and from balance. For a "seamless" blend — to use a word fa- vored by reviewers — all four bows must attack the strings in the same manner at the same distance from the bridge, must then be drawn over the strings at the same speed with the same pressure, and must be reversed from downbow to upbow and back again at the same moment. In such a perfectly blended sound, the first violin naturally emerges as the dominant voice, because it is the highest. Disparate bowings, on the other hand, produce four dis- tinct voices, so that the first violin's pitch is by itself less of an advantage. David Soyer of the Guarneri Quartet has remarked:

> In our quartet you'll often see everyone's bow doing something dif- ferent. We don't worry about visual similarity so long as we achieve aural similarity where appropriate.[55]

Here governance and personal relations in the quartet are causative. A perfect concurrence in bowing can be achieved con- sistently only in two ways: either there is strong leadership, or else democratic disagreements are softened by a strong mutual sympathy. A greater independence in bowing follows from a looser democratic consensus or from a more relaxed leadership.

The quality of the social relations within the group can also affect the balance of loud and soft between the instruments. Play- ers who are jealously guarding their own way, to use Samuel Rhodes' phrase, may be unwilling to get out of a colleague's way, even when it is the colleague whose voice the composer clearly wants heard above the others. The waltz that the Lafayette was rehearsing and debating in the second movement of Borodin's Second Quartet, for example, would be disrupted if the cello's broken chords were to be played as loudly as the first violin's melody. It would sound as if a hurdy-gurdy player had wandered off the street onto the ballroom floor. The cello part should sound instead as a blur of background harmony.

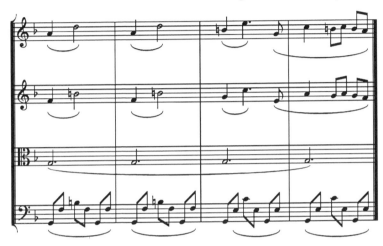

Yet there are some well established American quartets in which the jealous cellist habitually plays too loudly for much of the repertoire. It can be painful to hear the thin glass of Mozart shattered by a cellist's thumping out his notes at the basis of the harmony.[56] In some European quartets, one can hear the other extreme. Their sound is so perfectly blended, with the lower voices so slavishly conformed to the salient first violin, that the listener must struggle to pick out the lower three lines. The violist, especially, is drowned. Only when a cello solo emerges on the high A-string do the quartet's colors separate from the blur.

A quartet's sound is also influenced by the placement of the instruments in the players' semicircle. Seating the violist beside the second violinist in the middle of the quartet, with the cellist on the outside, facing the first violinist, as the Lafayette does, juxtaposes the inner voices and frames them with the outer voices. The result is a more tightly concerted sound. This is the seating, therefore, most favored by European quartets.

second violin   viola

first violin   cello

Many American quartets prefer the opposite configuration, with the cellist on the inside, between the viola and the second violin. Here the inner voices are separated while the cello's sound is more straightforwardly projected; on both counts, the result is a more delineated voicing.

second violin   cello

first violin   viola

The Lafayette chose the first of these two alternatives in part because of the difference in aural balance.

Ann: I like the sound of quartets much better when the two inner voices are sitting in the middle. I prefer the sound of the Borodin Quartet, the Alban Berg Quartet, the Quartetto Italiano.

Pam: I do, too.

Joanna: So do I.

Ann: Whereas the other way, with the viola on the outside — I feel that it's not great stereo. It's not as blended, and I personally like more of a blend, so that the voices are not so distinguished, except in places where they're meant to be —

Joanna: Right —

Sharon: Right —

Ann: — in which case we tend to project in a slightly different way.

Whatever choices have been made concerning placement and balance, any quartet player would agree with Ann that the sound must change with the music. What works for Mozart may not work for Schoenberg, or for Beethoven. Especially for some twentieth century quartets, in which the composer has weighted the voices with absolute equality, a separately voiced "American sound" is clearly the more appropriate. Elliott Carter, for example, has said of his intent in his four string quartets, which the Juilliard has championed:

> The four players are each his or her own individual, and all are aware that they have different characters. But they come together in an interesting way.[57]

A performance that projected a perfectly blended "European sound," with a first violin soaring above a gently adoring accompaniment, would hardly have caught Carter's point. Beethoven, too, in his late quartets, sought a radical equality among the voices, and to this day I feel that the Juilliard Quartet's fiercely energetic interpretations remain among the best.

For a listener, what sound to prefer is finally a matter of taste, and perhaps also of habit, since one may prefer simply what one has heard most. (It is only recently that I have come to prefer a more blended sound.) For performers, the right sound is the object of a lifelong search, and nothing is more irritating than to be told by a listener that the path of the search has been predetermined by geography or training.

> Joanna: When we've played in Europe, the fact that we studied with the Cleveland Quartet has branded us as an American quartet. But when we say our coach was Rostislav Dubinsky, then people go, "Oh, the Borodin Quartet, aha! European sound!"
>
> Ann: And yet the Cleveland Quartet didn't have an "American sound."
>
> Joanna: Who does?
>
> Pam: The Guarneri.
>
> Ann: The Juilliard. A big-boned kind of quartet sound. The Guarneri worked very hard with Alexander Schneider, of the Budapest Quartet, and Schneider had that. We played for him once and we got a little glimpse of that kind of coaching. It's big, thick quartet tone, completely the opposite of the Alban Berg Quartet, which we also coached with.
>
> Joanna: The Alban Berg, right, which is Austrian, or some of the Czech quartets. Everything is so light —
>
> Ann: And sweet—

Sharon: Subtle.

Joanna: Supposedly the American sound is: technical perfection and a harsh sound — people used to call it the "New York sound."

Sharon: You do hear that sound. I just heard a concert with that. It was in my face. A projecting, I'm-a-soloist sound from the different players.

Joanna: But there's an amazing confidence that's also involved in that kind of sound. And to say it's merely American is a stereotype. It's like, Americans are loud, Americans are direct, Americans are outgoing, whatever, friendly, and Europeans are more reserved. That's just a stereotype.

Ann: When we've been in competitions in Europe, we've heard people wanting to peg all the Americans as sounding a certain way, and when you go to England, they say that the Continent has a certain type of sound. And we Canadians feel, you know, we have that Nordic—

Sharon: We have that Caucasian sound, too, I bet—

Joanna: That's ridiculous. The fact is, I can't tell you how may times we've been asked: "Would you describe the sound of the Lafayette Quartet?" And we always say: "Well, we don't have a sound."

Ann: No. We do have a sound. I think a very special sound. A warm sound.

Pam: Well, for me at least, it stems from our training with Dubinsky. For one thing, it's using the same bow arm, the same bowing, to make the same sound.

Sharon: We work toward delineation of each voice, but we want to try to blend with the same exact sound. If Ann's at the tip of her bow, we're all at the tip for a certain note.

Ann: It's a very blended sound.

Pam: We talk about sound a lot and we're growing all the time with it. But to talk about the Lafayette Quartet's sound is hard, because we haven't defined it —

Joanna: No.

Pam: — as something to go after together, except in moments. And I hope we sound different when we play Beethoven from when we play Ravel.

Ann: Can I say, too, that I think the players define the sound, and I think that if the Lafayette Quartet didn't have me in as a first violinist, or didn't have any one of us as a player, the sound would change.

The Lafayette has yet another stereotype to play against: the proposition that quartets whose players are all women must — on the theory that women are experts at listening — make a recognizably concerted sound. One California concert presenter, for example, alleged in its announcement for a recent season: "To perform string quartets demands empathy, complementarity, and fine precision of response. Only recently did the world of music recognize that in these traits women excel."[58]

Ann: I'd like to see that brochure. That's a double whammy.

Joanna: I don't see how you can be objective with that kind of a comment at all. Listening and liking a group is purely taste. I can't say women play better together than men.

Pam: In orchestra auditions now, you play behind a screen so they can't tell. I'd like to go to some concerts where there was a screen up and I didn't know if the quartet was all female or all male, and then we could start making some judgments.

Stereotypes aside, a quartet's actual sound certainly emerges from the individual players, as Ann said — as surely as the accents of a speaker's voice are shaped by the speaker's personality. Although the Lafayette plays without a leader, it is unified by the strong sympathy that binds its players as people. Free of the antagonism that troubles many quartet democracies, the Lafayette moves naturally toward a blended sound. At the same time, Ann avoids the "European" extreme that subdues the other voices beneath the soaring first violin. Her solos in the Lafayette are distinct without being overbearing. Deeply expressive and necessarily virtuosic as her playing is, it does not dominate the quartet because dominance doesn't tempt her as a person. Sharon, for her part, contradicts the tradition of the shy second violinist, and she matches Ann as a swimmer stroke for stroke when the music calls for it.

Joanna practices the ironic detachment — the objectivity, to use her word — that serves violists well, since the voice of their instrument must be the least assertive. Yet she doesn't play with the dryness that is sometimes favored by violists; for the music she draws upon a warmth that in conversation she hides beneath a personal reserve. Her colleagues, in turn, are always willing — as some violists' colleagues are not — to get out of her way so that her solos can emerge into prominence from amidst the blend. Pam, finally, never competes to play too loud, but she has the determined will that cellists need to keep the pulse firmly as the bass in a quartet. At the same time she plays with the expressive ardor that cellists need as soloists. The result of these personal balances and contradictions is a quartet sound that is distinct from any other. It is blended and delineated at the same time. It is four, and it is one.

Sharon: For us, basically, it's always: you're going for the whole. I am not going to be a fantastic second violinist unless the performance of this quartet is fantastic. People might say, "Gee, wasn't that a great cello part in there, wasn't that a great viola part, wasn't that a great second violin part." But that's a byproduct. The main thing is that you have to sell the whole quartet, you have to sell the whole composition.

Ann: We don't want people to leave a concert saying: "I liked the viola and the first violin." We really don't want that. I think we've all tried to accomplish an equality of the four parts.

Sharon: There are a lot of quartets where the first violinist is the star of the show and the other three are just backup. Or the violist can't be heard.

Ann: Whereas our goal is that there's not one person out there, but that you're listening to four voices all the time, creating one story.

Sharon: One story, because we're all on one instrument. We just happen to be in different ranges.

Pam: The four-headed being that we are.

III. The Quartet as a Career

1. Beginnings

Sharon

Mine is a very simple story. Every Saturday night when I was grow-ing up in Cleveland, our whole family watched the Lawrence Welk Show. Wherever they had a little camera shot of the violinist — there were three male violinists and a female cellist in the studio orchestra — my mom would say, "Grampa played that instrument, do you like it? Do you want to play it?" And I was a yes-person as a kid, so I said, "Okay, sure." At eight years old, I took my first communion money, and we went down to Grabowski Music Company and for $140 bought my first three-quarters violin. On August 6, 1968, I had my first violin lesson, with Edward Matey, who was the last-desk first violinist of the Cleve-land Orchestra during the Szell years. I studied with him till I was fifteen, then switched to Linda Cerone. Also, from age eight to twelve I was in the Singing Angels, a hundred-person choir that toured all over singing barbershop and Broadway. I liked being in the limelight of it all, and I sang for lots of weddings — that was my part-time job starting when I was about twelve.

Near the end of high school, I started playing violin for gigs as well. At that point I decided to go into music, and I decided violin, because I thought it was more dependable. When I would sing on a Saturday morning for a wedding and my voice would crack, it was okay, I had a microphone, it was possible, but I couldn't imagine singing for a living. Violin seemed so much more dependable — you put your finger down and you get a sound. Of course, after your first couple of recitals you realize that the violin is not that dependable, you shake, your bow shakes, it's hard to play in tune all the time. But that's how I got into music.

I went to Baldwin-Wallace College in Berea, Ohio, in 1978, and then transferred to Indiana University after two years. I decided that if I really wanted to wake up and smell the coffee, I'd have to go to a big school and find out what a musical career is all about. There were 150 violinists at the school of music there when I arrived. You were surrounded by musicians from all over the world. I was twenty years old, and I remember being so depressed because just everybody seemed to be able to play concertos and do gymnastics on the fiddle, and I always felt behind. On the other hand, I feel like I had great work habits, that working class ethic, and I tend to be a very determined person, so if I set my sights on something, I try my damnedest to make it work.

I finished up my bachelor's in music and was already accepted into the master's program when my father, who is a foreman pressman in the newspaper business, lost his job because his newspaper went kaput. So I got a job teaching music history in the first year of the program, and for the second year, which was 1983-84, Rostislav Dubinsky offered me a job as his teaching assistant. I'd had coachings with him when I was first violinist in a student quartet in a chamber music course. For the assistantship, I was in charge of scheduling his coaching hours for the week and making sure that so and so was in such and such a group with so and so. I was his gofer and secretary and provided the grease for the hundred and fifty kids who came through his door. It was a situation where we eventually became friends. I think it's partly because of our similar backgrounds, Eastern European. He was Russian, of course, and my background is Polish on both sides.

I'd practice in Dubinsky's studio at night — I tend to be a night person, and some of my best hours of practicing were from ten at night to one in the morning. That was how I got to know Joanna. She had a key to Abe Skernick's studio two doors down, and she was a late nighter, too, so ten o'clock, eleven o'clock, she'd come by. We felt a little bit special, because we had studio keys to our teachers' studios on the first floor, while everyone else was scrounging around on the second floor trying to find a practice room. So she'd come and bug me: "When are we going to rehearse?" We were together in a gig quartet at the time. We played weddings, parties, anything that came along. Dubinsky wasn't coaching us at this point, because we were just preparing gig music, on as high a level as we could, but it was pop – the Pachelbel canon, Eine Kleine Nachtmusik. We didn't want to bother him with that. I was in a trio that year and coached with Dubinsky for it, and my solo stuff I would play for my private teacher, who was Henryk Kowalski.

Joanna and I decided we wanted to find another first violinist for our quartet, someone who wanted to practice and be serious about quartet playing and coach with Dubinsky. But we couldn't find anyone. Everyone we asked had their concertos or was concertmaster of this or that orchestra – they were prima donnas. It got to be October, November, and we still couldn't find anyone. Dubinsky knew of this plan, and eventually he said, "Well, would you mind – would you mind playing with an old man?" And of course we thought that was ridiculous. "We can't play with you, you have forty years' experience, and we have six months." But he said, "No. Come on, it'll be fun."

At the beginning of that year, in September, I'd had a big meeting with all the students who were in chamber music, to place them in groups, as part of my teaching assistantship with Dubinsky, who was head of the chamber music program at the school. There were the high level students, the middle of the road, and the mediocre, and you wanted to make sure that people were put in groups that could get along together. And a couple people I knew had told me about Pam Highbaugh. "You have to check her out, she's a wonderful cellist. Get her a good group." She had transferred from Hartt School in Connecticut and didn't know anybody at Indiana. Then in November, when we started playing with Dubinsky, the cellist we were already playing with got sick after two or three rehearsals. So we asked Pam to come in.

Joanna and Pam and I sat down with Dubinsky and made a game plan. We would learn the Shostakovich Third and Eighth Quartets and the Shostakovich Piano Quintet, which we'd play with Luba Edlina, who is Dubinsky's wife. We started rehearsing two or three times a week. Dubinsky arranged that we'd play at the Russian Music Festival at Sarah Lawrence College in May of '84. The Borodin Trio, which was Dubinsky's piano trio, was already scheduled to perform there.

It was only in the last six months of grad school that it occurred to me to be in a string quartet professionally. You know, you think to yourself: string quartets, that's a wonderful profession, but – me on stage? in front of 500 people? playing my part by myself? Forget this! I can't stand that kind of pressure day after day, week after week. And then, with Dubinsky, I realized that I loved it. I could already see that playing quartets would be a way to know myself better and know the world better. Quartet playing teaches you the most intimate things about yourself and the most intimate things about other human beings. I got totally caught up with that aspect of it. I'd probably have ended up as a psychiatrist if I wasn't a violinist. Quartet shows me slices of life that I'd never thought I could see. It's a great profession, to fantasize, to escape, to intellectualize, to wonder, to communicate, and to be intimate with other human beings. It's an amazing thing.

All this time, though, my last year at Indiana, I was taking orchestra auditions. I knew my symphonies, I had my Brahms symphonies down, a lot of Mahler symphonies, first violin parts, second violin parts — I would listen to a lot of symphonic works because I was trying to learn the excerpts. And I thought it was the greatest music. I did my auditions. I was a runner-up in San Antonio, in the finals in Cincinnati, and I was offered a position for a six-month stint in a Japanese orchestra. I also auditioned with Pam and Joanna for the Renaissance Chamber Players, which was a conductorless chamber orchestra being started in Detroit by Misha Rachlevsky.

To be honest, we really didn't know what hit us when we went to Sarah Lawrence to perform with Dubinsky. Here was our first chance to play professionally in the chamber music world, but we were not even really out of college yet. I remember so clearly. He took us on that plane, and we were like his three daughters, his and Luba's — they didn't have children of their own — and they were showcasing us. It was a wonderful concert — an incredible experience. Then my lease ran out in my apartment, we all graduated, and a few days after that we found out we'd all got the job in the chamber orchestra in Detroit. That job was for a whole year, instead of six months with the Japan job, and it was a lot closer, so why not stay in the Midwest? I called up the conductor in Japan and canceled. And it was in the Detroit job that we met Ann.

Joanna

My father's a jazz pianist and composer, and my mother taught piano at home when I was a kid in Seattle. I could go over to the piano and pick out all the songs that she was teaching, so it was obvious that I had a good ear for music. I wanted to be like the adults that would come over and play music sometimes. There was a woman who played the viola and I especially wanted to be like her, so I wanted to play the viola. But there wasn't enough money in my family for lessons, so mainly I just played in school, played for fun. In junior high there was a huge orchestra, and I think I got to principal second violin at some point, and in high school I kept on playing violin for my first year. There was also a conductorless chamber orchestra, and I thought that was a really good thing to be in, because you didn't have to have a teacher. They needed violists for the next year, so I just told them I played the viola and somehow weaseled my way out of auditioning. They just let me in. I didn't even know that viola parts are written out on a different clef. That was a shock when I came in the fall.

I was playing chamber music in high school and taking occasional lessons on the viola. I knew that I was really musical, and I could pretty much pick up an instrument and figure out how to play it, but I was more involved in theater, and I'd decided I was going to be an actor. During my last year, though, I started realizing I didn't like having to totally rely on everybody else, the way you have to in the theater, since if someone blew a line or their timing was off, you couldn't go off of it. I felt with classical music that I could just be on my own more, even though I was absolutely wrong about that — but I learned that later. After high school, I took a year off to work and rented a house and found some roommates, and I started to save up to study music. I'd already been working full-time since I was about sixteen — I'd done childcare, I'd done waitressing, was administrative assistant to a wind ensemble, worked in a record store, I'd been a cashier, an usher, a bookkeeper, I'd done all those things, but what I wanted was to play the viola. I knew I needed to go to a conservatory, because I knew I'd really have to practice a lot, since I had a lot of catching up to do. I committed myself to a musical career the day I decided to apply to the San Francisco Conservatory of Music, in 1978. At that point I felt like I really couldn't do anything else. I figured I'd probably never get in, but it was like anything else in my life — well, hell, I'll just throw it out there since that's what I really want to do, and meanwhile I'll just keep working where I am and see what happens. And they accepted me, with a full scholarship.

My first teacher there was a disaster. He kicked me out of the studio, told me I'd never make it. After that, I started studying with a violin teacher who friends of mine were studying with. He said he wouldn't accept me as a regular student, because he didn't teach viola, but he would give me a few lessons, and we really clicked. I ended up studying with him for a whole year before he said he would actually take me on.

This was Isadore Tinkleman. He was a very great teacher and had been a great violinist in his youth, but he had polio, so he had to stop playing. He had an amazing passion for the violin, and he turned that into teaching. There are players all over the place, in the big symphonies, in a lot of the young string quartets now, who studied with him. Tinkelman gave me two lessons a week, and he sent other students to spy on me to make sure I was working, because if I wasn't, then he wasn't going to keep on teaching me. But after a while it was obvious that he could teach me and I could catch on. I was supporting myself, but I also knew I had to spend that time practicing to get where I needed to be. And I did that. He could tell me things and I could get better very quickly, which is why I think he decided to keep me on.

I knew I was getting better while I was at conservatory, but I was always last chair in the orchestra. I basically had no status. My story is completely the opposite of Pam's and Ann's, because they had the training all their lives and they were always considered good players, being principal cello or concertmaster in student orchestras. I had the opposite experience. I was always fighting low self-esteem.

Chamber music was the exception. When I got to conservatory, I was immediately put in quartets with people who were much better than I was, because there was a viola shortage. The teacher who kicked me out actually pointed out that I was much more effective playing chamber music than playing a solo piece. First of all, it was technically easier, and second, playing along with other people was much more interesting and exciting for me than sitting there spending eight hours a week trying to play a solo piece and then eight other hours a week playing a scale or something like that. To me, that aspect was boring. I didn't get a big thrill out of playing a sonata or playing a solo Bach. I love the music and I could understand it well, but it just wasn't the same as playing chamber music. And then almost right away I started playing quartets for money.

I had a great teacher, I was making a living playing, I was spending my time studying and practicing, and I was too much involved in the present to think about the future. I just assumed that I would have an orchestral career and that I wouldn't be getting into a quartet, so I thought, well, what people do when they audition for orchestras is that they learn the symphony excerpts. I should probably go somewhere and study with someone who can teach me the excerpts. So applying to Indiana University was a natural progression. I made an audition tape, and I got in.

I was hired as a teaching assistant, and when I moved to Indiana at the beginning of the second semester, in January, 1982, I found out I'd been put in the second chair in the highest orchestra of the seven student orchestras. And this was someone who'd always been in the back, so I thought, "What am I doing here?" I was sure there was a mistake, because that wasn't my story.

When I arrived at Indiana, I was told, "Oh, shoot, we're really sorry about that assistantship we promised you, but we don't have the money." At that point I couldn't turn around and go back, so it was pretty shocking. I had already registered for classes, including Rostislav Dubinsky's chamber music class, and it looked like I would have to drop that to save on tuition. I went in to tell him. I was very upset, and he did his best to help me. He managed to get me a scholarship. So that semester I just took chamber music and orchestra and viola lessons with Abraham Skernick. I couldn't afford to do anything else.

Since I couldn't make much money playing gigs there, I had to get another straight job. I got work in a cafeteria, on the 5 a.m. to 1 p.m. shift, to avoid conflicts with classes. I had no car, and I had to walk to work. I'd get up at four o'clock in the morning and schlepp there in the snow — it's just beyond belief that I was actually doing this. In San Francisco I'd been making about twenty-five dollars an hour playing quartets, I'd had my own apartment, life had been good, and here I was now making three-thirty-five an hour. But when summer came, I went to the Spoleto Festival in Italy to play in the opera orchestra there, and I saved all the money that I made there, so when I returned I didn't have to work at the cafeteria.

I studied with Skernick for that first semester, and then when he took a sabbatical, I went on to study baroque viola with Stanley Ritchie, and I played in the baroque orchestra. Interpretively, that changed everything for me, in playing quartets, especially Haydn and Mozart. It may

105

be why I have such a passion for Haydn. Meanwhile I was working with Dubinsky; he was my chamber music teacher, and he helped me as much as he could.

The most important thing was meeting Sharon. She was in the same orchestra that I was in when I first got there, and I remember right away we were checking each other out, on the first day that we got in the orchestra, although we didn't actually play together until a year after that. She was kind of in the same boat that I was, in that she was not really considered top dog, and we connected on that level. It was during our second year of the master's program that we formed the gig quartet and then also started playing with Dubinsky.

Dubinsky had arranged some concerts for us for the spring, so we had something to work hard for, but I remember us thinking, "The year's going to come to an end and what are we going to do?" At that point, Sharon was not thinking about a chamber music career at all; she was definitely the orchestra-type person. Pam had always wanted to be in chamber music, and I wanted to, but I just assumed that it wouldn't happen. I auditioned for the symphony in Seattle, and Sharon had taken her auditions. Then I saw a job advertisement in the union newspaper for the chamber orchestra that Misha Rachlevsky was starting. His idea was, we would perform three times a week in the chamber orchestra, and then we would do chamber music concerts around Detroit. To me that sounded like a perfect job. I'd had experience in a conductorless chamber orchestra, and I was able to do quartets and quintets. I showed the ad to Sharon and Pam, and we all applied. We went to Chicago for auditions and then to Detroit for the finals.

Ann was at the auditions, and we all really liked her immediately, so we approached her at the audition and asked her if she would be interested in playing with us if we all got in. And we all did get in, although it was months before we were actually able to start rehearsing together.

Pam

In my family there was music. Both my parents had studied piano and had played for their churches as younger people. I have very early memories of singing in church and enjoying following the black dots long before I could read the words that we were singing. There just was an immediate attraction, and I begged and begged, seeing my older brother and sister getting piano lessons, to get piano lessons myself. It was family rule that you had to be eight in order to play, and I guess I was finally obnoxious enough that I got lessons earlier than that. My parents could see right away that I was very motivated. I really didn't have to be coaxed to practice. It was really just a part of my daily joy. After a while I switched to cello, and I soon began with Gloria Noble, who still teaches in Santa Clara, California. She is a great teacher, and her studio is still full of young cellists wanting to do something with their lives in music. I studied with her all the way through high school. I also played in the San Jose Youth Symphony. Eugene Stoia was the director, a Rumanian violinist who played beautifully, and he was very dedicated, almost tyrannical, though he was a sweetheart. He expected a result that was pretty amazing, I think, for youth groups.

It wasn't clear to me at this point that I would become a professional musician. When I enrolled at the University of California at Santa Barbara, I chose a double major involving sports as well as music. I love sports to this day. If you give me a softball game to play in, I'm as happy as I ever am. I went into ergonomics and was studying energy and coaching and thought of myself maybe being a coach and being a teacher somewhere, but through the medium of sports, instead of through the medium of music.

After my freshman year at Santa Barbara, I went to the Banff Music Festival. That was a key changing point. I studied with János Starker in his master class. I felt like I had to just wake up. What was it to be a cellist, really? I knew I wanted to be able to explore that part of myself that needs to express itself through the cello. Studying with Starker and hearing other cellists play, I realized that music was not some magical thing that happens — what's really magical about it is already there. But to make music happen, I could, just like anybody else, learn how technically to get it out. I could learn to get the tools. Starker's influence on the world of string playing, not just the cello, is profound. It's not only that he's scientific; he gives confidence. He teaches a holistic understanding of what you have to do to play. And it wasn't just that somebody who is smarter than somebody else can go from a low C up to a high C on the cello and nail it every time. It's that if you're prepared in the right way how to hear it, and if you can practice the timing with your bow, *you* can do it. It's a tool that you learn.

I spent a second year at Santa Barbara, and then went down to Cal

State Northridge in Los Angeles for three years and studied with Peter Rejto, a cellist who's a member of the Los Angeles Piano Quartet. He was my main advanced cello teacher; I learned to play the cello the way I play it basically because of him. He was the right teacher for me at the time, because he extended the thought processes I had begun under Starker: technique is only there to serve what you want to do musically. He was a teacher who'd thought those technical things all out. He'd tell me I needed to have this certain fingering at this certain point, and this was when to transfer the weight from one finger to the other. Or to get a more beautiful vibrato on this fortissimo statement would be a matter of analyzing down to what width of vibrato and how many oscillations — down to such technical, detailed understandings. It's not that you luck out or don't luck out, and it's not just through repetition; it's definitely that if you follow A, you'll get B.

I suppose the first thoughts about what I would do in my future professionally came while studying with Peter Rejto. I would talk about it, and he would just say, "Well, Pam, I think you're a chamber musician. You have that quality to listen and play." I wasn't the nerves-of-steel player. We had master classes every Thursday for three hours, and I would always get nervous, and so I don't think he felt that being a soloist was the best use of my musicality. I actually did a lot of concertos the last year in college, and I was starting to get confidence about that, but I just loved the quartet literature.

In the summer of 1981, one year before I graduated, I went to a quartet program in Troy, New York, that Charlie Castleman teaches every year, and that just did it for me. That seemed like the right goal. I was already playing in the Young Musician's Foundation Debut Orchestra in Los Angeles and in the Pasadena Symphony, and those were great musical experiences for me, and I don't think I ever put completely out of mind that I would want to play in an orchestra, but in an orchestra — I know that I'm just really particular about music, little timing things for example, and I wasn't very happy being in an orchestra where my stand partner next to me wasn't really feeling it with the conductor. Playing in orchestra would be like trying to dance in a dance company for me — not being able to do exactly what I wanted.

For me, music is a very very personal thing. Even to say it's been my best friend at crucial times would be a cheapening way of describing it. Music for me is that part of life where you connect with people far beyond this world. It's a beautiful pathway to understanding people, or at least the part of people that I want to know and be close to, which you might call their soul. That's what attracts me. It makes living have a dimension far greater than what I know just from eating and sleeping and driving a car. I think it's always been that for me, and that's what I want to be true to. I still want to study more, I want to understand why music moves me, rather than simply live on the fact that I'm doing okay now in a musical career. That's still what lights my fire, rather than wanting to play this concert, wanting to play that one. If I play it, I want to play it because I have something that I *have* to say, because I finally understand music more.

After I graduated from Cal State, I went on into the world of graduate schools, because I knew I needed to study more. So I studied at Hartt School of Music with Raya Garbousova for a year, in Hartford, then went back to LA to be Peter Rejto's assistant for a year, and then applied to Indiana specifically because it was a big enough school where I might just find some people to form a quartet. And I did. I met Sharon and Joanna. It was pretty amazing.

I met Dubinsky early on, but my real first exposure to him was playing in the quartet with him with Sharon and Joanna. That was thrilling. The concert we played with him at Sarah Lawrence was just embedded into my heart — some of the moments in the music with him. You knew there was someone who was leading you that had a lifetime of experience and a conviction for the music in a way that just made you play with him, you couldn't help it, it was such a rich opportunity. I knew it was one of the things I was going to count in my life as a remembered time. The three pieces we performed with him and Luba Edlina, the Shostakovich Third Quartet and the Eighth Quartet and the Piano Quintet, are at the very basis of the Lafayette Quartet's repertoire.

I had every intention of finishing my degree there at Indiana, and I actually was all set to be Dubinsky's assistant the next year, taking Sharon's job, because she and Joanna were a year ahead of me in the program. But then Joanna let Sharon and me know about the chamber orchestra that was going to be starting in Detroit, and Dubinsky had wanted us to keep this quartet together some way or another. I was actually in a second quartet as well at the time, and the other members of it wanted to continue at Indiana, but I felt much more compatible with Joanna and Sharon. They were very determined people, and I knew they wanted it as badly as I did. They would be willing to starve for a few years. And I think you get a sense of that pretty early on.

Ann

My mother's a concert pianist and my father's a university choral con-ductor and a composer, so I grew up in music. I began in the womb, listening to my mother play Brahms and Beethoven piano sonatas, and when I was a kid I heard a lot of choral music. That was my musical background. This was in Sackville, New Brunswick, which is seven kilo-meters from the Nova Scotia border. My home overlooks the Bay of Fundy. It was a remarkable place to grow up. A little English cultural center, 3,000 people when the university's in session, right bang in the heart of French New Brunswick. It's really Canadiana, old Canada. We Easterners consider places out here like Victoria practically the colo-nies.

I wanted to play violin, from the age of three, maybe two and a half. As soon as I was big enough to stand on a chair and put a record on, I always put on Mozart and Beethoven violin sonatas and Bach Brandenburg concertos. I wore the records out. And so I talked my mother and father into letting me take violin lessons. I didn't have my mother's abilities, though. My mother was a child prodigy. I wasn't a child prodigy. I didn't think about being a professional violinist. I wanted to be a ma-rine biologist, or to work with horses. And even today, those are my two things that call me. If I did for some reason lose the ability to play the violin, I would probably want to train horses and dive all the time.

I studied with Pauline Harbourn, who has a tremendous gift for teach-ing younger players. Then, when I was seventeen, I met Victor Yampolsky. He was the man who changed my life, in terms of the direc-tion that I was going to take. He was conductor of the Atlantic Sym-phony Orchestra, which is now Symphony Nova Scotia. He'd been a student of David Oistrakh, and he'd been the principal second violinist and the associate conductor of the Moscow Philharmonic. So he had a lot of musical integrity, also coming from his father, who was Oistrakh's accompanist. At this point I was going into the eleventh grade, and I needed a new teacher. My old teacher in Sackville was wonderful, but I needed somebody much more demanding, and she was actually the one who showed us an article about Yampolsky moving to Nova Scotia.

After I began working with him, I would travel to Halifax every Saturday or Sunday with my mother or father. We'd drive to Halifax and drive back, two and half hours each way. A lot of parents think a forty-five minute drive for their children is a big deal, but my parents said: "Of course we're going to drive to Halifax." And I looked on it as a normal thing. Now I have students coming to me from Courtenay and Nanaimo way up Vancouver Island, an hour and more away, and I realize that they don't think anything of it. It's good; I like it when parents think that.

I worked with Yampolsky for seven years. He's a truly brilliant violinist, a much more thinking violinist than I am. He started gearing me to become more technically adept. A sense of intonation, a sense of vibrato, a lot of things. He and my mother were my two artistic mentors — my mother more instinctively, since I grew up hearing her practice every day. That and what Yampolsky taught me are now coming together. I was doing really hard things back then for Yampolsky, and it's not exactly that I'm better now on the violin, but that I know what I'm doing now. I was always pretty good, but I didn't know why or how I was doing it. I think that frustrated Yampolsky a lot, because from week to week he would have to teach me the same thing.

When he moved to Boston University, I followed him. My parents couldn't possibly afford to send me, but I got a full scholarship. By that time, I basically knew that I had to do music. I had no choice. Yampolsky was already convinced that I should be a musician and that I could make it as a violinist, and I realized that I couldn't go through life without doing this, without playing violin at the level that I was playing. I'm a Capricorn. It's got to be this level or not at all.

I'm not saying there was an apocalypse. The sky didn't open. But I think it was Yampolsky. It was his influence over me, my love for him as a teacher, my admiration for him as a musician, his ideal of perfection. I would go for a lesson for one and a half to three hours every week. And he was so picky, although he was very generous at the same time — the real Russian school of teaching. He never ever gave compliments unless he felt they were really strongly deserved. So there was a tremendous amount of needing to prove to him that I could do it. I needed that. Even now, when I sit down and play in quartet, I have to play well. I have a real strong sense of pride, and I'm scared to walk into a quartet rehearsal and not sound good. I want people to be moved by what I do.

111

When I was studying with Yampolsky, I did not want to be a string quartet player. I wanted to be a soloist. Yampolsky was definitely gearing me for a solo career, or else for chamber music. But at the time he didn't say chamber music, and he never said orchestra. He did make me work with a wonderful pianist, so he never discouraged my chamber music. But when I would take orchestra excerpts to him, he'd say, 'You shouldn't be learning this,' which made me think 'Well, I've *got* to learn it.' But the feeling I got from him was: you're not going to be doing orchestra. I think he saw my lack of interest in it from the beginning.

When I was a student, I was never happy in an orchestra, never satisfied. I always had some form of physical ailment that I'm sure manifested itself because of my unhappiness in being stuck wherever I was in the first or second violin section. I would get back pains. I would hang off the edge of the bed trying to get rid of them. Orchestral life — is "subjugate" the right word? You are no longer responsible for the artistic output. You are a cog in a wheel. You must play beautifully, you must play fabulously, if you're going to be a great orchestral player, but ultimately you're doing what somebody else has decided you're going to do. But for me, quartet has become the most personal and most wonderful way of exploring myself, exploring my way of expressing myself through the most intimate form of music. You can't get that in an orchestra.

While I was at college, I was learning concertos every year, playing recitals every year. I played concertos with the orchestra there at Boston University a couple of times and had a bit of a solo stint performing concertos in New Brunswick. I did a lot a gigging. But I didn't have that tremendously powerful urge that you have to have to be a soloist. It's something that's beyond just a great talent. You also have to have what it takes to be an Olympic athlete. And I was never a real big egoist. I'm not saying that all soloists are egoists, and I have a big ego myself, but it isn't that driven kind. I work much better in a group situation, hearing other people's comments: "Work on it this way."

I guess there was a turning point when I spent a summer at Tanglewood, when I was working with Yampolsky there and also playing chamber music with other students for the first time. We played the Dvorak double bass quintet, which I loved, and the next year we worked on the Debussy quartet. Before that I'd had hardly any experience playing chamber music. Then I met the two people who did the most to change my feelings with regard to chamber music. One was Eugene Lehner, who'd been the violist in the Kolisch Quartet. He was seventy-something when he used to come and coach us at Boston University. The Juilliard Quartet coached with him; he's had that kind of influence in the musical world. He's had a huge impact on whoever has worked with him. He's always looking for new ways of expressing himself; his ideas are always growing: that's what moved me.

The other influence was Diane Pilafian, who was the violist in the Primavera Quartet, which lasted for nine years. During my last year at B.U., I heard her play a big solo as principal violist in a chamber orchestra; they were playing a piece by Bernstein. And I remember thinking: This is not an ordinary gigging violist, this is a real musician playing here. I was just struck by her playing, because it was so different, so remarkable in the way she used her bow. The American school of playing is a lot more strident, a very stiff kind of playing, but I had been taught the opposite of that by Yampolsky, and here was this violist playing that way.

My teacher used to say: "You're pooshing. Pooshing." He'd always be running to his dictionary, thumbing through to find the right words. "Ah, 'poosh.' Poosh. Don't poosh." And there is this kind of element in the Russian sound, this kind of freedom in the bow arm, using the whole bow. If you push, you do get a big sound, but it's so — grrr, it can grate on your nerves after five minutes. You kill the sound with the weight of your arm. The sound I learned takes a lot more control and a lot more practice because you have to keep your bow very straight. The volume's the same, but the sound doesn't have an edge to it.

Diane Pilafian had the sound I wanted for myself. I went up to her and introduced myself after the concert — which was an unusual thing for me to do then, because at that time I was still a little shy. We struck up an amazing friendship, and I started playing quartets with her, with me on second violin so that we were the two inner voices. I studied violin with her whenever I could. I would just try to imitate this understanding of quartets that she had. Now this is where, I think, part of the history of the Lafayette Quartet begins, because Diane's quartet, the Primavera Quartet, had worked with Rostislav Dubinsky at Indiana. He had coached their Shostakovich Eighth, all their Russian repertoire. So Diane played quartets like Dubinsky, using the whole bow, that same fluid kind of style that I had been studying with Yampolsky. And during the same year, Sharon and Joanna and Pam were already studying with Dubinsky at Indiana, although of course I didn't know them yet.

I met my colleagues the next summer, when I was in Boston after graduation, trying to think of what to do. I got a call from Yampolsky, who had heard about the job opening in Detroit. The idea was that half the time we'd be playing in the chamber orchestra, and the other half of the time we'd be playing quartets, trios, quintets, and duets. What could be bad with that? It sounded like a perfect job, although it turned out not to be at all, for a whole lot of reasons. But the great thing about it was that during the auditions there, I met my colleagues. They heard me play, and they came up to me and said, "We're a quartet, and we're looking for a first violinist." They told me they had been playing with Dubinsky for a year, but of course that had been temporary. And I knew about Dubinsky through Diane. So I said, 'Okay, great. Let's be a quartet.'

The Lafayette Quartet

Ann: We were in the chamber orchestra in Detroit for a little under two years. Joanna and I were roommates, but I never saw her except in orchestra rehearsals, because she was working ninety hours a week. I wasn't working so many hours, because there were six violins, but there were only two violas, so she had to perform more chamber music. It was pure slave labor. Misha Rachlevsky, the director, didn't allow us to perform together as a quartet as part of the job, and there seemed like no way the four of us could sit down and rehearse quartet music after rehearsing all day and night with his orchestra and his chamber groups.

Finally, in May of 1985, near the end of our first season in Detroit, we sat down and said, "Are we going to play quartets, or not?" We decided to do it. So on top of everything else that we were doing, we started meeting at 8:30 in the morning to rehearse, or at 8:00 o'clock at night. Nobody in the chamber orchestra knew that we were working on quartets together. We started with the Haydn Opus 20, No. 2. I think that was my idea. I'd learned it with Eugene Lehner. Then we did Shostakovich's Eighth, which they'd played with Dubinsky, and I'd learned with Diane Pilafian, who'd also learned it from Dubinsky.

After we'd been rehearsing in secret for about two months, the chamber orchestra went to a summer music festival in Vaasa, Finland. Without telling Rachlevsky, we arranged for our quartet to play the Haydn Opus 20 during an all night concert — an 8:00-p.m.-to-4:30 a.m. marathon they do every year. At 3:30 in the morning, there were still five hundred people there milling about, and they stayed around for us. They liked us. Afterward the director of the festival came up to us and said, "You guys are going to do something with your lives." That was our first performance.

When we got back to Detroit after the summer, I knew I wasn't going to stay with the chamber orchestra. It had become more and more intolerable for me. Misha and I did not get along. He said I had too elaborate a bow arm. By the end of it, I couldn't play at the tip any more, I couldn't use the whole bow. And the concerts were awful. There were so many train wrecks. Missed entrances, rushing, missed intonation — if we did those things now in quartet, I would refuse to get up and play. All of us would.

That year, 1985, in December, Oakland University in Rochester, Michigan approached us and asked us if we would consider being their quartet-in-residence. The appointment gave us the use of a van and a tiny bit of money for teaching and a few odd jobs here and there — for instance, playing at dinners. That was our residency at Oakland University, but still, there was suddenly an institution behind the Lafayette Quartet. That was the first legitimizing thing that happened to us. And we started doing more and more concerts in schools, and we had our own series in a little meeting room on the ground floor of the Lafayette Towers, an apartment building where by that time I was living. That's how we got our name.

Pam: The name was my idea. We'd been looking for a name for ourselves, and we'd gotten nowhere with it. But just driving to rehearsal at Ann's apartment one day, I saw the Lafayette Avenue exit sign, and we were playing in the Lafayette Towers, so I thought, why can't we make it the Lafayette Series with the Lafayette String Quartet?

Ann: I finally resigned from the chamber orchestra in February of 1986. I'd been offered a teaching job by the Center for Creative Studies, an inner-city music school, and my parents were saying, "Why stay in this job?", and I'd met my future husband, Bob Goldschmid, and he was helping me. My colleagues were intending to stay with the orchestra until September and then resign, because the music school was ready to hire them, too. And finally they did it, they left the orchestra.

Sharon: We were already talking about jumping ship, but I was the last one to say yes. At one point I even suggested to the others that maybe they should start finding a different second violinist. I wasn't sure that I was ready to give up financial security for a pipe dream, which is how I thought of striking out on our own as a quartet. I want high goals, but I tend to always do whatever's within my realm. I tend to be very earth-bound. And I remember very clearly sitting on my bed in a motel room in Wickson, Michigan, talking to Dubinsky on the phone with this letter of resignation in my hand, and I couldn't decide whether to send it. Dubinsky was saying, "Sharon, this'll be the smartest thing you've ever done in your life. You have to keep the quartet." Then I got on the phone with my parents, and I love them dearly, and they were saying, "WHAT? Leave your job? You're a musician and you get paid every Friday and you're going to leave it? Who the hell do you think you are? What, are you going to pitch a tent outside in Detroit, Michigan?" There I was with this wonderful good-Catholic be-stable foundation — and to dream! That was a big transition for me. I did jump ship. I knew I had this generous guarantee of $5,000 a year teaching Suzuki method at the Center for Creative Studies. I got my VISA card in the mail and I was jobless. It was July 21, 1986, and we became a full-time quartet.

Ann: Absolutely nobody I knew or had even heard about had done the things we were doing, breaking away from an orchestra job, which was paying $13,000 or $14,000 a year at the time, and dropping our salary by more than half so that the four of us could just play quartets.

Pam: I knew Sharon wasn't sure, since she'd never really dreamed about playing in a quartet to the same extent that I had and Joanna had, so it was a bit more of a process of change for her during that second year with the orchestra. I knew I wanted it, and I was trying to convince her. We'd already had a similar kind of musical nourishment with Dubinsky, which had brought us together in the first place. And after we quit the orchestra, we went right away and worked with him, and we felt liberated, because we could use our bow arms, we could make free with the bow, and that was our secret, the glue that held us together.

116

Sharon: We were also at the same part of our lives. One of us did not have three babies and a big house in the suburbs. There wasn't an inequality in age, in finances, in status, as there is in a lot of quartets. And we'd also been in the same job together for two years.

Pam: That was another glue for the four of us, knowing what could happen in an ensemble, as opposed to what we wanted to have happen.

Sharon: After we left the orchestra, we made a two-year pact. We said we would give it our all for two years. And a lot of times I operate by this I'm-going-to-bang-my-head-against-a-brick-wall-and-make-sure-it-gets-done theory. I'm a little calmer than I used to be, but I was bound and determined that these other three people whom I was going to rely upon, not just financially, but for a career, that they were really going to stand by what they said. And they have. And I think that's why I tend to be sometimes too exuberant, but, if you look at what's happened with us — after just six years, we were playing two concerts back to back on the Concertgebouw stage in Amsterdam. It was like the Cinderella story for me. We got out on that stage in Amsterdam, and I remember just looking out there and thinking, "Oh man, I never expected — Wow!" Now I look at any student or any person who has in their head an inkling of a dream, and I say, "Run with that ball." That's how people should live.

Joanna: When I think about it, I kind of scratch my head — you know, how the hell did I get here? Because from what I was doing even ten years ago, I wouldn't have imagined what's happened with us since. Things have always had a way of falling into our laps. A few days after we resigned from the chamber orchestra, we got a call from one of the local pianists, who used to work in Munich in the summer at the International Institute for Chamber Music. He was on the faculty at Oakland University and we'd played a couple of concerts with him, and he told us that the Munich festival needed string teachers. That was basically the start of our career, right then.

Ann: It was our first big job as a quartet.

Pam: We were asked to come at the last minute. The instrumentalists that were supposed to come refused to fly to Europe that year because of the Chernobyl accident. We were young and stupid, so we said, "Okay, if we die by terrorism or whatever, it's fine." We went because it was a great opportunity to teach. It turned out they had a whole bunch of students from Taiwan. It was all charades of course, because none of them spoke English. The idea was that we would coach the student groups through the first three weeks and then the Alban Berg Quartet would come along and teach the last week. As it turned out, that gave us an opportunity to play for an established quartet for the first time. All of the members of the Alban Berg coached us in turn. It was tremendously important for us.

The cellist, Valentin Erbin, and I instantly struck up a camaraderie. It was probably at a time in my life when I needed a role model of some sort. My colleagues and I hadn't been a quartet that long, and the thought of myself truly being a quartet player in a professional way was still a dream. And then Valentin spoke about his feelings, about how it took twenty years for him to even think that his quartet was well-known, about how nervous he would be in a concert hall — he was so human and easily shared his thoughts with the kind of love and devotion for music that I enjoy. In his coaching, he kept talking about extending your limits, and it was again, I suppose, the same feeling I had with János Starker and Peter Rejto, that they were saying it's a lifelong process, but you can figure out a path.

Ann: I think the biggest impact that the Alban Berg made on me personally at the time was listening to them rehearse. The detail with which they would practice was so amazing to me. It was so exacting. I learned a lot about practicing string quartet music. I remember listening to Gerhardt Schultz, the second violinist, practicing a downward fifth, two notes, just this: *daa,* dum — over and over, one hundred times. You could just barely hear a subtle change in vibrato, or perhaps in bow speed. Then later you'd hear it in their concert, and it would be just magical. He wasn't satisfied with it just one way. He drilled it into his body and be able to do it one hundred different ways. Each one of them had in their repertoire so many options for all of the little things that they have to do in their parts, so that if at any given moment in performance, they heard one of their colleagues playing it in any way, they'd be able imitate it.

Sharon: At this point, we'd already met Sally Sanfield. She was an artists' manager in the Detroit region. We needed a manager to arrange concerts for us and negotiate fees. Obviously we're not going to up to people and say, "How about if you presented us for a concert, for such and such a fee?" Wedding gigs we could arrange for ourselves, but for concerts, negotiations, publicity materials, we wanted someone to represent us. We played for Sally, and she decided to take us on.

Pam. She did a lot for us those few years.

Joanna: We could say to her what we felt our career needed, and she would meet it. If we needed X amount of dollars, she'd say, "Well, school concerts is where we have to go." So then she'd get us a bunch of school concerts.

Pam: We would do ten or twelve a week sometimes. It was very well organized. It was good for us to have a chance to play, to try out new pieces, to have the experience of talking to students. Meanwhile, because of the relationship we'd established with Oakland University, giving us the name "artists in residence" long before they were able to give us any money, we were able to apply for grants.

Joanna. We had some local patrons, and eventually we also got a grant from Chamber Music America, which is the professional association for chamber musicians. We got a Ford Motor Company grant as well.

Sharon: Before that, during our first six months, I remember, we made $6,000. It was laughable. I think we ended up paying ourselves $800 apiece out of that $6,000, after expenses. That was the hardest part, trying to stay together and have enough to live. The only lot of money we were sure of was the $5000 or $6000 from the Center for Creative Studies, and the rest was gigging, true gigging. Our sacred rehearsal time was 11:00 to 2:00, but if any one of us could find a gig for $50 or more, and she could say, "Hey, you guys, I have this studio gig, it's from 9:30 to 12:30, could you please...?" So: "Okay, sure, no problem, let's change rehearsal, we'll work around it." That was an unspoken agreement between the four of us. We had to pay our own bills in order to keep the quartet together. If that meant changing rehearsal so that someone could pay her electric bill, fine.

Joanna: The studio gigs were usually night shows in Detroit. Dionne Warwick.

Sharon: Bob Hope.

Pam: Tony Bennett once. It was just a pick-up orchestra. Very nice people. I remembered we'd already started "I left my heart in San Francisco," the footballs for that — that means the whole notes — laying out the harmonies, and the violins had little scales —

Ann: Which were never together. But it sounded okay.

Pam: And then Tony Bennett came on kind of suave, and started humming it in mid-bar, before breaking out into the big song. We were all just spellbound.

Sharon: Those moments. As much as you play quartets, I got goose bumps from that.

Ann: It was never a decree of the quartet that we would stop doing gigs. Each individual person came to that on her own, according to her needs, when she could say, "I don't need to do this any more."

Sharon: The Christmas before we went to Victoria, 1990, that was my last gig. It was $300 — I remember, because I was going to buy a sofa with it.

Ann: In my recollection, that early time was frustrating in many many ways. We hadn't worked out a way of communicating. We each had our own idiosyncrasies that none of us really accepted in each other yet. It wasn't nearly as good as now in many respects. For every hour of rehearsal, we spent two hours talking, discussing, calming somebody's hurt feelings, discussing how we could rephrase something so that somebody wouldn't feel hurt the next time it was said.

Sharon: And we were teaching so many hours. Twenty-seven hours a week.

Ann: Any Suzuki kid who could walk through the door. And we were teaching in two institutions, sometimes three. Often I wasn't home till 9:30 or 10:00 at night.

Joanna: When I look at my life in Detroit compared to now, all the driving I did, an hour and a half a day at least, and how broke we were — I lived in an apartment that was probably about the same size as my studio now, and it was not in a great neighborhood, with a train track right next to me and a freight train going by all the time. I was unhappy, unhealthy, a lot of things. But I stuck with it because what was happening in quartet was making my life worthwhile.

Sharon: Eventually the two-year-pact idea dissolved. No one even thought about stopping after two years. We were playing concerts, mostly in the Detroit area, we were rehearsing three hours a day, we kept coaching with Dubinsky, and we were starting to enter competitions.

Joanna: I was the one who was pushing us into the competitions. I'd played in competitions before, and I knew they would be a way for us to distinguish ourselves. We sent a tape to Young Concert Artists, and it was rejected, and we entered Fischoff National Chamber Music Competition in 1987 and didn't even place, but the next year we entered again and ended up winning the first prize and the grand prize.

Sharon: Two thousand dollars.

Pam: That seemed like a lot at that time.

Ann: The Fischoff got us a tour, too. It legitimized us for the first time in the States. And the next year we won the Chicago Discovery Competition.

Joanna: In 1988, we placed third in the City of Portsmouth International String Quartet Competition, in England. It was strange in a way, because they were very open about not expecting much from four women. I remember the outfits we had on — black skirts, and two of us with long-sleeved red blouses, two of us with blue blouses — and they just looked at us and said, "No. These guys are a joke." And they were quite surprised by how we ended up playing.

Sharon: You enter the competitions to catch the eye of a national manager who will promote you and arrange concert tours, but the funny part was that before we went to the Portsmouth, Mariedi Anders had already signed us on. That was another one of those little crossroads that would validate us. "Oh, you have a manager? *Oh,* Mariedi Anders!" And all of sudden instead of little prep schools, we were taking tours to New York City and California.

Pam: Then in the same year we won the Cleveland String Quartet Com-

121

petition, which gave us a scholarship to coach with the Cleveland Quartet for two years at the Eastman School of Music in Rochester. We didn't exactly win the competition. It was kind of magical. I read about it a couple of days after the auditions had closed. But I had played for Paul Katz, the cellist of the Cleveland Quartet, and had actually been accepted by him to go to graduate school there, but then went to Hartt School instead. So on the strength of that I just got up my courage and called him and said, "I see that your competition has already happened, but I just wanted to tell you that I'm in this quartet now, and we were kind of wondering if there were any options for us coming to work with you sometimes." And he said, "Isn't that funny that you called, because five minutes later I would have been walking downstairs to talk to the dean. We had the competition, but we really didn't decide that we wanted to take any of the quartets. So tell me a little bit about the Lafayette Quartet." I told him about the quartet, and later as he was walking into the dean's office, who was there but Charlie Castleman, the director of the quartet program that I had been in four summers earlier, in Troy, New York. And since Paul had only heard me play for twenty minutes or so, he said, "Charlie, do you remember Pam Highbaugh?" And Charlie said, "By all means, listen to their quartet."

Sharon: What he said was, "Any quartet that Pam Highbaugh is in, you've got to listen to."

Pam: Paul and his colleagues agreed that we could come and play for them, and they took us on. But they also had another group that had been in the competition that they wanted to work with as well, so instead of our moving to Rochester, we came in once a month, and that gave us the freedom to keep our teaching jobs in Detroit.

Joanna: The scholarship paid for our tuition and travel.

Ann: The Cleveland Quartet sort of took over where Dubinsky left off for us. We were still going to Bloomington to play for him, and that was always really special, but his thinking was on a different level. Dubinsky didn't deal with the intricate problems. Maybe he'd say, "You're playing too fast." But usually he'd just sing it and we'd play it and it worked. On a purely musical level, Dubinsky had the greatest impact on us. The Cleveland's influence was more nuts and bolts.

Joanna: Soundmaking and counting. Rhythm and sound.

Ann: Donald Wallerstein especially, who was the Cleveland's first violinist at the time, was just so picky. He would sit there and have us counting. He would just never give up. He would get each one of us individually to play our part over and over and over again until he was satisfied. He'd explain in different ways; he was such a wonderful teacher in terms of patience.

Sharon: With the Cleveland, for the first time in my life, I was playing not concertos or sonatas for a teacher, but second violin parts for Peter Salaff, a second violinist who'd known the parts for twenty years.

Pam: The Cleveland Quartet helped us tremendously, and as people they were very supportive, in showing what it really is like to be in a quartet and how they worked things out as human beings. We would complain how busy we were, and they would say, "Yeah, but the more concerts you get, it's going to only get worse, you guys, it never gets better." And they still recommend us in many ways. Our job in Victoria is somewhat because of that.

Sharon: Victoria was like a meteor from outer space. But that happens to us. Pam came in to rehearsal — it was October of 1990: "You guys, a man called from the University of Victoria School of Music, looking for a string quartet." I said, "Where's Victoria?" Joanna said, "Oh, we used to go there for vacations. It's right across Puget Sound from Seattle."

Ann: We were already actively looking for a move. We were seeking to leave Detroit, and were actually looking to California. We had a very good opportunity there which fell through just before we were offered the residency in Victoria.

Sharon: They had called Chamber Music America looking for quartets that might be interested, and Paul Katz, who was president of the organization then, recommended us. They called Bob Silverman at the University of British Columbia, and it so happened he had played with us, and he recommended us. It seemed like wherever they turned, they heard the name "Lafayette." When they first called us, we rolled our eyes and told Pam to tell them thank you, but no thank you, because it was so far away. But then they called again, and eventually we decided to go.

Joanna: Every one of us felt very differently about going to Victoria. Some people had strong doubts. I had doubts about its being an island, because I'd always been tied to big cities. But as far as the job went, I had no reservations. Sure, I was ready to see if I could make it work. This is the highest standard of living I've ever had in my life, right now. I don't have to worry every month about how I'm going to pay my bills. I'd been in that situation, literally, since birth. That had been my existence. So for me this opportunity was amazing.

Ann: A residency like the one we have in Victoria is a solid position that legitimizes us as artists outside of the performing. There are all sorts of different residencies, of course, and we've had others, mini-residencies, longer ones, but this is an ideal one, because we get a salary and benefits, which relieves us of a tremendous amount of the problems that young quartets have that don't have a residency. It carries a lot of responsibilities, but we're lucky to have it.

Joanna: And if we weren't involved in teaching, we wouldn't be helping to keep music performance alive, and it's not only the performers. A lot of people we've taught won't end up performing professionally, but hopefully they'll continue to love music as a result of the work that they've put in, and then they'll be the ones that go to the concert hall. I think that's one reason so many classical musicians teach, because by passing on exactly what you do, you're keeping music alive.

Ann: By professional quartet standards, we see ourselves as still relatively unknown. We're finding that, particularly in Europe, our career is just now beginning to sprout. Because we won a prize at the Portsmouth Competition, we were invited to play at the Orlando Festival at Kerkrade in the Netherlands, and we met people there who've helped us. We've played in a lot of the major halls and festivals in Holland, and now we're playing in Austria and England and Italy as well. We have managers in Holland, England, and Austria, as well as the U.S. Slowly you add to the countries where you're beginning to be known. That aspect of it, the chance to perform more, in more beautiful halls, for more and more sophisticated audiences, is really a wonderful thing to look forward to.

Joanna: Just being part of a tradition. That's very exciting.

Pam: Basically, we're striving for greater competence, and always for that deeper look inside music. The true validation of your work is what you yourself feel that you've produced. But when we do have opportunities to play in the great halls of this tradition, it helps, because it's another way for us to know that we're on the right track.

Sharon: It's like a little flag you put up. "Okay, we've made our debut at the Concertgebouw, at the Mozarteum in Salzburg, and Wigmore Hall in London. We've gone through all those." And now we're ready for the next thing, whatever that may be.

2. Team Music in Mass Society

Stardom

In modern society, we usually associate success in an artistic career with the achievement of fame. The famous writer sells the most books; the star diva sings in the most prestigious opera houses for the highest fees. There is nothing new in this. In classical music, the tradition of the celebrity virtuoso and the star singer already existed before 1700. But while the members of the Lafayette Quartet look forward to greater professional success, they do not expect to achieve it through stardom. The careers of string quartet players follow a different path. Their music is written for colleagues, not for stars. It celebrates cooperation and discourages individual display. When the players on stage face each other rather than the audience, stare at their scores, and lean into their instruments, their demeanor, like their music, effaces the solo personality and places teamwork in the spotlight. As a result, individual members of quartets rarely become famous. Audiences fill large halls to see star soloists, but, as individual personalities, quartet performers in their anonymous dark dresses and suits are no draw at all. Quartet audiences take little notice of the names, ages, nationalities, and personal histories of the players. Many listeners have heard of the Juilliard, the Guarneri, the Tokyo, and the Kronos Quartets from the United States, the Borodin from Russia, the Lindsay from Britain, the Alban Berg from Austria, but the members of these famous ensembles are entirely unknown to the public as individual musicians. Almost no one among their audiences can list them by name.[59]

Quartet performers are, in general, content with their anonymity. Teamwork is what lured them to quartets in the first place. Players who yearn for the limelight are usually waiting to change careers. Two former members of the Cleveland Quartet relate:

James Dunham: My daughter came home from school one day saying she'd happened to mention what I do, and one of the teachers had gotten all excited and said, "Oh my gosh, I know that group, they're so famous!" And my daughter had said, "I guess that's right." She said to me, "I don't think of you as famous, though." And I said, "Well, I don't either."

Peter Salaff: The funny thing is, the same thing happened to me. My son asked me — he was very excited — "Dad, are you famous?" — "Well, I don't know. I never really thought about it."

James Dunham: That's not high on our list of things to think about.[60]

From a celebrity entertainer, even from a classical soloist, such a protestation might well ring false, but from a chamber musician it is merely natural.

Ann: The music we play doesn't beg for star status. It's not ever active with that kind of adulation, like with a soloist. If we were to be stars, we'd be four stars, not one, and that's an awkward concept for most people.

Sharon: We had a touch of that at a summer festival. "Oh, we can't live without you. Oh, here's the quartet!" — that kind of situation. It didn't feel right on us.

Joanna: Nah. The kind of ego, the kind of strokes you need to be a soloist or a conductor, is something that absolutely does not interest me. Even if I played the violin, I wouldn't want that. That wouldn't be my lifestyle choice.

Pam: When I was studying, never was I hoping that someday I would have a CD and that people would know me when I walked into a store in the city I live in. That never crossed my mind. My wish was, "I hope I get chances to play music. I hope I get to get out there." And the great halls are exciting, because the audiences who come to them are just as appreciative of what we're doing as we are to play there, but it's no more important to me to be able to play in the Mozarteum in Salzburg than to just be able to play in my parents' living room, ultimately.

That quartet players do not become stars puts them at a disadvantage in the modern economy, where products are marketed by the promotion of brand names. We are used to the entertainment industry selling celebrities in the same way that the cosmetics industry sells shampoo. The singer's famous name is the brand, and the famous face is the advertising logo. In classical music, concert presenters and recording labels promote conductors, opera singers, and instrumental soloists with splashy photographs of star faces attached to famous names. In response, audiences buy concert tickets and recordings. But star marketing is of little use to quartets. Their celebrity is always limited by the absence of a single star face and star personality.

There are, of course, exceptions. The Budapest Quartet became famous in the United States, and the Kronos Quartet has become famous as well. The celebrity of both is due in part to qualities that star marketers can exploit: the Budapest's flamboyance, and the Kronos's preference for hip clothing and mood lighting. More important to their unusual fame, though, is that both groups have stood out as innovators. The Budapest was the first quartet to successfully export string quartet performance to the American hinterland though indefatigable touring and through broadcasts. It was also the first of the great quartets to experiment with democratic governance. As for the members of the Kronos, they are pioneers in commissioning and performing post-modernist music, including quartets by third world composers, jazz and pop composers, and minimalists. But celebrity such as theirs is rare. In general, quartet music lacks the star-making qualities necessary for a mass art. Therefore, it can never be much of a money-maker in the mass economy.

Survival

As a result, it is almost impossible for professional quartet players to make a living from performing alone. The ruthless calculus of the public concert will not permit it. Quartets cannot compete with star instrumentalists who play recitals in 3,000-seat opera houses. The arithmetic of such a recital might be this: the concert organizer that is presenting the star in the opera house charges $30 a ticket and sells all 3,000 seats. The gross receipts for the concert, therefore, total $90,000. The concert presenter can afford to pay the soloist a $35,000 fee, and still have enough left over to cover the hall rental, a backlog of overhead, and the deficit incurred in half a dozen other concerts. Of course, from most of the 3,000 seats in the opera house, the recitalist is a speck on a cavernous and otherwise empty stage, and the sound of her instrument is heard far more faintly than it would be in a small hall meant for recitals, or on a recording. No matter. The point of going to solo recitals in huge halls is not after all to listen to music, but to see the celebrity perform. We can then hold her image in our minds when we actually listen to her play on a recording at home. The soloist, meanwhile, out of her $35,000 fee, pays her accompanist $5,000 and her manager the usual 20 percent of her $30,000 share, or $6,000. Her net is $24,000 for the evening. If she plays 50 such concerts a year — a modest number for a touring performer — her income, before expenses, will be $1.2 million.

Quartet audiences, though, do not go to concerts to see stars, but to hear music. People who organize and present classical concerts agree that of all their audiences, quartet lovers are the most devoted to listening. They are an audience that can be counted on to come to a concert even when they've never heard the name of the performers. Otherwise, the Lafayette would never have been able to fill the church for its concert in Mill Valley. But the corollary is that quartet audiences are not often willing to fill a large hall to hear a performance. They don't want to be looking at specks making distant sounds. Thus even the best known quartets end up playing most of their concerts in recital halls of no more than 800 seats. And such concerts do not permit a high fee. An 800-seat hall sold out with tickets costing $25 — already high for a chamber concert — brings the presenter $20,000, not $90,000. A few of the best known quartets can fill large halls — especially if the halls are known for superb acoustics, like Carnegie Hall in New York — and for these concerts quartets can charge as much as $15,000. But in most halls, for most concerts, even the most celebrated quartets earn much less.

For their concerts in the United States, the best paid quartets usually earn from $7,000 to $12,000, depending on the city and the size of the hall. Quartets in mid-career, like the Lafayette, meanwhile, can charge $4,500 to $6,500. Younger quartets can earn $2,000 or $3,000 if they have just won a competition prize; otherwise, even less than that. Concert fees for quartets can range a little higher in Germany and Japan than in the United States; in other countries, they are lower.

Even the middle range of these fees, around $6,000, may seem high for a night's work, but it is not. In the first place, a quartet's fee must be divided into five equal shares. Each of the four players' share is a fifth; the other fifth must go to their manager. (In classical music, managers are not what their name suggests. They are booking agents, fee negotiators, and advisors, much in the manner of literary agents for free-lance writers.) Once the manager's commission is paid, further expenses must be deducted before the individual musicians can receive their shares.

For chamber musicians in the United States, an average of forty percent of performance income is consumed by travel costs alone, according to a 1992 survey of 1,120 American chamber ensembles conducted by Chamber Music America.[61] Travel is made more expensive by the need for separate hotel rooms so that the musicians can practice. Quartets, moreover, need a fifth airplane ticket for the cello. Publicity materials, printed music, office costs, foreign taxes, instrument insurance, and instrument mortgages require further deductions. Managers attempt to arrange "block bookings," which reduce the cost of travel by moving the musicians on tour in a logical progression from east to west and north to south. Tours are nevertheless exhausting and expensive. For North American quartets, touring internationally is more a labor of love than a source of earnings. Playing closer to home can make money, but only the best paid quartets can expect to return from abroad having done much better than break even.

The result is that a mere thirteen percent of professional chamber musicians based in the United States earned more than $10,000 in 1991 from performing in their ensembles, according to the 1992 Chamber Music America survey. Half of the ensembles that responded to the survey reported, further, that they had no health insurance.[62] In 1989, the music journalist David Rubin persuaded six American quartets, four of them in existence for over ten years, to open their books as an anonymous but public demonstration of the hopelessness of string quartet performance as a sole source of earnings. The six quartets played, respectively, ten, twenty-six, seventy-five, forty, one hundred, and sixty-eight concerts in 1988. After paying their travel costs and their management's commissions, but before deducting other expenses, the first group lost $3,700, while the other five earned $19,000, $37,000, $28,000, $152,000, and $190,000. These balances had to be split four ways. Thus even the $190,000 earned that year by the most experienced and highest paid of these quartets probably resulted in a net of some $40,000, before taxes, for each of the four players. Nearly ten years later, fees from performance have risen slowly, while expenses have risen rapidly, and Rubin's study, if repeated now, would probably report even lower net incomes.[63]

Alternatives

Since it is almost impossible for quartets in North America to make a living from performances alone, almost all are actually part time performers. Many quartet members are moonlighting symphony players. As quartets, they may give ten to twenty concerts a year, most of them in or near the city where their orchestra plays. Other quartets jump ship from their orchestra jobs, as the Lafayette did, to become independent touring ensembles. They are free to play fifty to a hundred concerts a year. For them, financial security comes from employment as artists in residence at conservatories and universities.

It is not only quartet players who teach, of course. Almost all performing musicians are forced to earn part of their living by teaching. The exceptions are celebrated soloists and players in the most prestigious orchestras. Fortunately, musicians do not usually consider teaching a form of blood sacrifice. Unlike the more solitary artists in literature, sculpture, photography, and painting, musicians in every classical tradition understand it to be part of their professional responsibility to rear their own successors. They themselves have progressed in their careers through a series of mentors. Their lifelong reverence for their teachers compares only to that of disciple for master in traditions of spiritual practice. Both traditions are passed on from teacher to student, one to one. (Classes with one student are expensive. In modern universities, the only students who cost more to train than musicians are doctors.) Most musicians begin teaching their instrument to children when they are still students in music school. They continue to teach during the height of their careers, even when they do not need the money and are often on the road. Nor do they stop teaching after retiring from performance. Eugene Lehner, for example, the violist of the Kolisch Quartet, who in his seventies coached Ann's student quartet, continued to teach well into his eighties. His tirelessness, far from rare, is typical of his art.

Therefore, the Lafayette's acceptance of a university position does not mean that its members have resigned themselves to mediocre expectations as performers. Playing quartets before the public is still their professional mission, and if some of their time and energy is spent with students instead, their situation is little different from any other chamber ensemble's. Almost all of the most celebrated contemporary North American string quartets — the Tokyo, the Cleveland, the Orford, the Juilliard, the Emerson, for example — hold, or held until their retirement, faculty appointments in music schools. As many other universities and conservatories have done in the past fifteen years, the University of Victoria School of Music hired its quartet to attract ambitious string players as students and to provide the students with a living example of a successful chamber music career. The Lafayette teaches part time, to leave room for rehearsal. When the musicians are on tour, their graduate students fill in for them. The quartet has also established a summer festival for student quartets and has begun to sit on competition juries. Each player accepts a few students privately. Meanwhile, they continue to play about fifty concerts a year.

In Europe, chamber musicians have greater freedom. Audiences are more numerous there, and the concert venues are closer together. Most European quartets are based in one of six countries that are relatively small in area and that have strong string quartet traditions — Germany, Austria, Hungary, the Czech Republic, the Netherlands, and Britain. In these countries, concerts for local music clubs and in provincial town halls make it possible for quartets to perform more often than their North American counterparts and yet spend more of their nights in their own beds. Government support of musical performance, too, is more significant in Europe, both through grants to concert presenters and through engagements of performers to broadcast on state radio. (In this respect, as in others, Canada is a European country. The Lafayette is often heard on the CBC.) European quartets, then, do not need the same support from music schools. Except in Britain, their employment as artists-in-residence is much less common than in North America.

In Canada and the United States, string quartets teach, and meanwhile, as performers, they must choose between two alternatives. Either they join orchestras and play quartets in their free time, or they join a faculty. Otherwise, after the first few frazzled years of weddings and studio gigs, the collapse of their group beneath financial pressure is inevitable.

Historical: Quartet Performance in North America

One reason that playing quartets is a more precarious profession in North America than it is in Europe is that quartets have been a European habit for far longer. Quartets have been heard in Europe since the 1770's, and professional ensembles began forming in Beethoven's time. In eighteenth-century

America, meanwhile, the elites were aware of quartets, as they were aware of European aristocratic culture in general, but very few Americans could play the music. It was only during the latter half of the nineteenth century that classical music in general became popular in North America. By this time, however, European taste favored solo recitals, operas, and symphonies, not chamber music; and North American taste followed along. Many frontier cities built opera houses where audiences could idolize touring divas and instrumental virtuosos. Orchestras were also being established as professional musicians immigrated from Europe or were trained by immigrants. The New York Philharmonic was founded in 1842, to be followed by the St. Louis and Boston Symphonies in 1881. But string quartets were rarely heard in these years.

Only after the turn of the twentieth century was the first full-time professional quartet in the United States founded. It was the Flonzaley, established in 1902 by Edward J. De Coppet, a Swiss-born New York doctor. (De Coppet was not a member of the quartet, but its patron, as was his son after him.) The Flonzaley Quartet was preceded in Boston by the Kneisel Quartet, established by the Romanian-born Franz Kneisel in 1885 with other members of the Boston Symphony Orchestra. The Kneisel went full-time in 1903, a year after the Flonzaley. But relatively few North American audiences heard them perform.

After the First World War, as composers led a revival of chamber music, a new generation of performing string quartets was formed in Europe. Working in alliance with composers, many of them championed the dissonances of the new modernism. The Kolisch Quartet, for example, dazzled audiences, and even more their fellow musicians, by performing the Schoenberg quartets from memory. But performers were best able to attract new audiences to string quartets by playing older works. They programmed the quartets of Mozart, Beethoven, Schubert, and, Dvořák. These were composers whose symphonies audiences were already used to hearing, and it was from them that listeners learned to appreciate the sound of team music. Even now, despite a gradual acceptance of modernism, music written before 1900 still dominates quartet programs.[64]

Audiences after 1918 came to accept quartets only slowly, despite performers' willingness to play the old masters. The musicians were, after all, proposing a radical downsizing of musical forms — from hundred-piece orchestras to four-piece string bands. Audiences are rarely ready to accept without hesitation the changes in taste that artists propose to them. But in this case there were other, extra-musical reasons for their reluctance. Symphony orchestras and opera companies had become economically entrenched. The patrons were committed, the institutions dominant, the halls built, the musicians' career-investments made. The audiences, besides, were loyal to their favorite repertoire — which was, after all, none the less powerful because other kinds of music were now being written. Chamber music eventually became established with classical music-lovers in large part not by converting symphony-goers and opera-buffs, but by finding new audiences. There is still very little overlap, both in Europe and North America, between subscribers to symphony concerts, to opera seasons, and to chamber music series. As single-ticket buyers, and especially as record buyers, listeners can be eclectic; but as subscribers, they tend to cherish particular loyalties.

In the decades between the world wars, quartets were brought to the United States by European ensembles on tour. Americans heard the Pro Arte Quartet from Belgium, the Kolisch from Austria, the Griller from Britain, the Hungarian from Hungary, the Budapest from Russia, the Busch from Germany, and others. In the 1930's and 1940's, several of these quartets settled in the United States or Canada, in some cases to escape Nazism. By exception, the Hart House Quartet, which carried the quartet repertoire into the Canadian hinterland during the same period, was founded in Toronto. In both countries, these pioneering ensembles developed the stamina to travel by train among cities that were not tens of miles apart, as they were at home, but hundreds of miles or thousands, and to play for audiences that had never heard a string quartet before.

Their work was supported by new forms of institutional patronage. The Hart House Quartet was granted a twenty-year subsidy by the Massey Foundation in 1925. Beginning in 1940, the Budapest performed regularly at the Library of Congress for an annual stipend. The Pro Arte was hired as faculty at the University of Wisconsin in 1940, the first quartet to be so hired in the United States, and the University of California followed in 1949 with its faculty appointment of the Griller Quartet.[65]

These and other quartets — as well as individual string players whose ensembles did not survive the war intact — trained a new generation of North American performers. After 1945, quartets composed entirely of young American musicians gained international recognition for the first time. Most notable were the Juilliard Quartet, founded in New York in 1946, and the Fine Arts Quartet, founded in Milwaukee during the same year. They were followed by still younger quartets: the New York-based Guarneri, for example, began its career in 1964; the Toronto-based Orford Quartet started performing in 1965.[66] The public became slowly aware of the quartet literature through recordings and radio broadcasts and, above all, through the growing number of concert series.

Public attention turned decisively to chamber music, however, only under the impetus of economic and social change. With gathering speed after 1960, symphony and opera audiences were moving to the suburbs. Metropolitan orchestras and opera companies, married to their great halls, could not move with them. A handful of chamber music societies had long been sponsoring quartet concerts in cities. Now many more sprang up in the suburbs, staffed by volunteers who did not relish a trip into town for concerts on weekday evenings, but who found they could lure musicians to the suburbs on Sunday afternoons instead. (In founding the Candlelight Concerts, which I attended as a child in the Connecticut suburbs, my father and his friends were among the pioneers in this movement.[67]) For the new suburban concert presenters and their audiences, quartets and instrumental recitals were suddenly the most accessible musical choices. No suburban hall could accommodate an orchestra, even supposing there was money to pay an orchestra's fee.

Thus, for the first time since the public concert hall had eclipsed the aristocratic salon in the early nineteenth century, quartet musicians had an audience designed precisely for them.

Sometimes they were reduced to playing in dead and drafty high school auditoriums. But more often they found themselves in eighteenth- or nineteenth-century Protestant churches on the edges of pre-suburban village greens. The contemplative associations of these church-halls, their warm and clear sound that reverberated in the choir lofts, and their seating for no more than two or three hundred listeners combined to make them, as it turned out, ideal venues for performing and hearing quartets. This happy chance is one significant cause of the quartet's subsequent popularity among North American audiences. Protestant churches continue to be the site of chamber concerts throughout the continent, and for listening to quartets there are, in general, no better places anywhere.

The Chamber Music Boom

By 1975, North America was prepared for what came to be called the chamber music boom. It resounded among all the participants in musical activity: audiences, performers, composers, concert presenters, artists' managers, music schools, recording labels, and donors. Beginning in the 1970's, the number of professional string quartets exploded. There were twenty-seven professional string quartets in the United States in 1965; by 1992, there were 179.[68] A separate count shows fourteen professional quartets in Canada in 1993, of which ten were based in orchestras and four were full-time — one in New Brunswick, one in Quebec, one in Ontario, and the Lafayette in British Columbia.[69] Of the 1,120 professional chamber music ensembles counted in the United States by Chamber Music America in 1992, ninety percent had been formed since 1980.[70]

The new interest in chamber music among performers arose partly in response to a change in public taste, which created a new demand, and partly, too, in response to the dearth of employment in orchestras. Openings in secondary orchestras now attract hundreds of applicants, most of whom are good enough on their instruments to qualify. Students in music schools say they have be a Heifetz to get hired to take a seat among the second violins. For instrumentalists graduating from music school in the 1980's, like the members of the Lafayette, forming a chamber ensemble, however risky, had become a plausible career alternative.

Music schools have gradually responded to the changes in the musical marketplace. In 1979, San Francisco Conservatory established a masters degree program in chamber music performance, the first such program in the United States. The Indiana University School of Music, the largest of its kind on the continent, began its chamber music program in 1981, and most schools have followed, often hiring string quartets as resident teachers. The participation of music schools in the chamber music boom has institutionalized it. By creating secure employment for existing ensembles as artists-in-residence, the schools ensure the ensembles' survival. They also guarantee the production of a new generation of chamber musicians as their teachers' eventual competitors and successors.

In the revival of chamber music performance, string players have been the lucky ones. They can draw on the inexhaustible quartet repertoire and can build upon an attenuated but never broken tradition. But quartet players are by no means the only participants in the chamber music boom. Only sixteen percent of the professional chamber groups counted by Chamber Music America in 1992 were string quartets.[71] Many young pianists have abandoned solo careers, or hopes for one, to join with string players or with each other to form touring duos, piano trios, and piano quartets. Singers have taken the a cappella chamber literature of the Renaissance and the Middle Ages on the road. Wind and brass players, in ensembles of various sizes and compositions, have revived the outdoor-music repertoire of eighteenth-century composers renowned and obscure. They have rearranged pieces composed for other instruments; have championed the music of Hindemith, Poulenc, Carter, and other modernists who have delighted in winds; and have petitioned and commissioned composers to write new music for whatever combination of instruments their ensembles happen to be.

In response, rescued from their academic isolation by these eager young performers, composers have poured forth chamber music in a variety and profusion unequaled since the death of Mendelssohn. Chamber Music America estimated in 1992 that 3,000 compositions had been commissioned by American chamber musicians during the previous five years alone.[72] Although it was the modernist composers who revived chamber music after the turn of the century, younger composers who have moved away from modernism have by no means abandoned chamber forms. American minimalists such as Philip Glass; recreators of medieval spirituality in music, such Arvo Pärt and John Tavener; composers who combine prepared tape with live acoustic performance, such as Steve Reich; and those who combine Western and non-Western musical traditions, such as Terry Riley, Lou Harrison, and Tōru Takemitsu — all have written for string quartet. The quartet has also invaded improvisational forms: the Turtle Island String Quartet, from Berkeley, and the Uptown String Quartet, from Harlem, play jazz. Modernism may be gradually retreating into history, but neither composers nor performers are content to let the quartet retreat along with it into another period of obscurity.

The popularity of quartets eventually had an effect on government policy in the United States. Although governments in Canada and Europe have long supported chamber music performance, there was little public funding for chamber music in the United States before 1980. In part to persuade granting agencies to think otherwise, Chamber Music America was formed in 1977 as a professional organization of performers. (Organizations that present concerts were added to the membership in 1979.) During the 1980's, funding from governments, corporations, and foundations was built into the institutional structure of chamber music performance. Composers received commissions supported by grants, and performers secured grants for residencies and tours. The most significant role of public and private funding, though, continues to be its support of organizations that present concerts. According to Chamber Music America, there are now 1,400 chamber music presenters in the United States, and sixty percent of them were established after 1970.[73] Few of these organizations, new or otherwise, could continue without outside funding. Ticket sales typically cover only half of a concert presenter's expenses. Grantwriting and fundraising make up the rest.

The creation of teaching residencies in music schools and the doubling of the number of concert presenters have had the effect of disseminating chamber music throughout the continent. Professional string quartets are now resident in thirty-two American states and six Canadian provinces, including such once-unlikely locations as South Dakota, West Virginia, Hawaii, New Brunswick, and Newfoundland.[74] Audiences can still hear more chamber music in New York City than anywhere else on the continent, but the power that New York, Boston, and Toronto long held over classical music has been dispersed. Fewer than a third of chamber concert presenters in the United States are now located in the Northeastern states.[75] The ambition of the earlier quartet pioneers to plant their music in the hinterland of North America has been realized.

After the Boom

During the recession of 1989-92, classical music ceased to grow rapidly as a non-profit industry. During the subsequent economic recovery, chamber musicians and their supporters found themselves in a struggle to keep intact the far-flung structure of concert tours, grants, and teaching residencies that they set in place during the 1970's and 1980's. The boom quieted. Classical music performance has now entered a period of ominous stasis.

For performers, the most evident effect is an end to the growth in the overall number of concert engagements, on both sides of the Atlantic, due in part to a decrease in government support of concert presenters. In Europe, where concert presenters are heavily reliant on government money, funding cutbacks, even in countries as devoted to music as the Netherlands, have forced presenters to cancel concerts. Already more parsimonious than in Europe, government support in the United States has declined even more sharply — most notably at the national level, where Congress has come to view the arts with hostility. Funding from private sources in the United States — foundations, corporations, and individuals — has meanwhile remained stable — preferable to a decline, but nevertheless a retreat from thirty years of steady increases. Only in one economic sector, that of local government, has support for the arts continued to grow.[76]

Further, while the number of concert engagements is no longer increasing, more performers are competing for them, as music schools continue to propel new graduates into an already saturated market. Among quartets, so many excellent ensembles are now touring, in competition not only with each other but with a new profusion of wind quintets, brass quintets, piano trios, and others, that supply has overtaken demand. Only the most celebrated quartets can now count on booking all the concerts they want.

Whether the classical music audience itself has shrunk is a matter of debate. American audiences for all the arts declined slightly during the 1989-92 recession, but they have again reached their former numbers. According to a 1993 study commissioned by the National Endowment for the Arts, 21.5 million Americans attended at least one classical music concert in 1982, and 23.2 million in 1992 — in both years, about one eighth of the adult population. Growth in the arts audience, as a whole, has apparently leveled off.[77] Of seven "age cohorts" identified in a follow-up study, people aged forty-seven to fifty-six in 1992 attended classical concerts in the greatest numbers. Younger people attended less often. The preponderance of people over forty-five can, of course, be observed at any classical concert in North America. The major question for the future of classical music performance seems to be this: will people born after 1955 — once their children are grown and they have more time and more money to spend — imitate their elders and come to concerts more often? Or will their childhood immersion in pop music, movies, and television keep them at home, with the result that classical performance will begin an unalterable decline?[78]

At present, audiences for chamber music in the United States remain stable, as they are for all the arts. But this overall stability represents an average. In fact, the loyalty of audiences varies considerably, according to one important factor: who is presenting the concerts. Forty-one percent of presenters responding to

Chamber Music America's 1992 survey reported that their chamber music audiences had grown, while twenty-four percent said their audiences were shrinking; the rest reported no change.[79] There is, therefore, a wide difference among chamber music presenters in how well they are maintaining their audiences.

The cause of this difference is not location or size. Successful presenters exist in every corner of the country, whether they are large, professionally managed concert organizations in metropolitan cities, arts-sponsoring programs connected to universities, or smaller volunteer-run concert series in suburbs and towns. What distinguishes these successful groups is the skill, the vigor, and the musical sophistication of the individuals who run them. The common elements are commitment to the repertoire and assertiveness in the recruitment of audiences. Presenters that flourish have adopted the marketing techniques of mail-order merchants: phone banks run by volunteers, purchase and exchange of mailing lists, slogan-splashed color brochures offering discounts and deals. Adaptable presenters schedule concerts at times and places convenient to middle-class workers. San Francisco Performances, for example, one of the most innovative of professional urban presenters, stages hour-long concerts at 6:00 p.m. in a restaurant in the city's Financial District, with free refreshments. Suburban commuters can attend before going home, instead of having to return to town in the evening. San Francisco Performances has also presented its string-quartet-in-residence, the Alexander Quartet, playing the Beethoven cycle on Saturday mornings at Fort Mason, a popular Bay-side park, in sold-out performances. Like many other presenters, San Francisco Performances seeks to train new audiences by hiring musicians on tour to visit public schools and community music schools. The students are offered free tickets to the performers' evening concert downtown.[80]

By contrast, panic at the temporary decline in concert attendance during the 1989-92 recession led many presenters, especially those connected to universities, to abandon their audiences instead of recruiting them. They scrambled to replace solo recitals and chamber concerts with ethnic dance, world music, and jazz, which are easier to sell to young people. But the better managed presenters have not found it necessary to forsake classical music. Cal Performances, for example, a program of the University of California at Berkeley, is one of the oldest and largest concert presenters in the country. Its director, Robert Cole, has stated the case for the continued presentation of chamber music concerts:

The widespread idea that chamber music doesn't sell is totally fallacious, and the many university presenters who have stopped presenting chamber music are not paying attention to their audience. People say that the audiences are getting older. But it's always been that way. It's not a new phenomenon. When I was in my twenties, the audience was older. In our chamber music concerts, the student population is rather small, even when we go all out with publicity. But it doesn't matter if there are only twenty students there with their free tickets out of 700 in the hall. They're the concert audience of the future. We serve the students in so many other ways — with the world music and dance programs.

Our core audience for chamber concerts is our faculty and emeritus faculty and their friends. A large number come from the sciences. Many are retired, but then, the old are demographically the fastest growing group. They're the ones who have time to come, and since they're more mature, they're more interested in chamber music. With string quartets, you see the interaction as it happens, and so there's an intellectual and a human side — instead of an impersonal delivery from a star, which seems to have more value to the young.

Besides, we have to raise money. No one has been able to survive in this business by ticket sales since around 1970. And who gives the most? The chamber music audience. Why shut off the spigot of your best supporters? But most of my peers can't hear this — except some of the younger ones.

The real reason so many university presenters aren't presenting chamber music is that they aren't musically aware. They don't see, for example, that the string quartet audience is the most devoted, most musically aware audience that exists — the most focused on music. The repertory is beloved by the public, and presenting it makes economic sense. I can sell four or five or six string quartet concerts a season, and at the same cost to me as one orchestra.

Presenters who can't see all these realities are going out of business. Some people say it's harder in the smaller university communities. But that doesn't explain why volunteer presenters are successful in smaller communities all over the place. They've taken the market away from other presenters who don't understand the business.[81]

A similar view is taken by C. Richard Lemon, who with his partner John Kongsgaard manages Chamber Music in Napa Valley (California), one of the most distinguished volunteer presenters in the United States.

I know there are presenters that are turning away from chamber music, with the idea that they have to follow their audience or lose it. But I would be surprised if anyone who is committed to chamber music and who feels it, instead of just reading about it, actually has trouble attracting an audience. In fact, I think it's the other way. I think people are leaving less personal art forms for chamber music, because as things get more complex, worldly, and collective, we're all trying to seek some more personal connection with the spirit. I think chamber music is stronger in that.[82]

My own view is that audiences will continue to be devoted to the string quartet, just as composers and performers are. The quartet is a unique invention, and nothing seems capable of replacing it. It was no accident that it was created at the beginning of the industrial revolution. Even in Haydn's day, the quartet was a deliberate affirmation of the beauty of human relations at a time when traditional social forms were disintegrating. During the second half of the nineteenth century, when factory and empire served as engines of hope, the quartet seemed less important, and when World War I undermined confidence in industrial society among thinking people, quartets again became an attractive musical paradigm. In our day, the quartet speaks even more strongly of the healing power of live human interaction on a small scale, in contrast to the depersonalization and virtualization of mass life. Quartets distill and preserve our common humanity. While the music lasts, we are affirming that we can work and live together in harmony. In the words of the American composer Martin Bresnick,

The string quartet is like a paradigm of the most utopian aspirations of human beings. It is the model of human cooperation as we all hope it could be — each individual contributing his or her mite to the totality of the vision. It represents what will have to be the future of our species if we're going to survive.[83]

Appendix A

A Listener's Guide to the Quartet Repertory

If this book has moved readers to explore the terrain of string quartets more widely for themselves, the guide that follows may help them. In these pages, the best quartets of the great composers are listed in chronological sequence and briefly described. The list reflects my own preferences, of course, although much of it represents a general consensus. As a further reduction in the number of choices, I have proposed, at the end of the guide, a list of twenty best of the best.

1. The Viennese Tradition

Josef Haydn (1732-1809)[84]

Opus 20, No. 1-6 (1772)
Opus 33, No. 1-6 (1781)
Opus 50, No. 1-6 (1787)
Opus 54, No. 1-3 and Opus 55, No. 1-3 (1788)
Opus 64, No. 1-6 (1790)
Opus 71, No. 1-3 and Opus 74, No. 1-3 (1793)
Opus 76, No. 1-6 (1797)
Opus 77, No. 1-2 (1799)

Haydn wrote sixty-eight string quartets, far more than any other of the great composers.[85] The forty-four listed above lie at the foundation of the quartet repertoire.

The composer arranged almost all of his quartets in groups of six. The only exception, among the groups listed above, is the last, Opus 77, which consists of two quartets only. In the first two of these groups, published as Opus 20 and Opus 33, Haydn is still learning. As for the thirty-two quartets in the later groups, all are masterpieces. For a listener wishing to negotiate this overwhelming abundance, I recommend beginning with the last eight quartets — those of Opus 76 and Opus 77.

The six quartets of Opus 76 are — to consider them together as a unit, as they should be — among those works of art that sum up the achievements of a great artist at the height of a long career. Everything that Haydn knew how to do better than anyone else, whether before him or after him, is displayed in these six pieces. The first movements are thrilling, the slow movements sweet and lovely. The triple-meter movements (the minuets and trios) and the finales are witty and inventive, and they focus the listener's attention on the art of composition itself at its most brilliant and masterful. The six pieces should be listened to in the order in which the composer arranged them, as an album. They are rarely performed that way, unfortunately, but are easily obtained as a group on recordings.

One can easily imagine why Haydn left Opus 77 unfinished after two entries in the series. It was not only that he was busy with the oratorios that dominated the close of his career. Once the first two quartets were written, it must have dawned on him that there was nothing more that needed saying. Opus 77 No. 1, in G major, and No. 2, in F major, are entirely unlike the six of Opus 76, which had been published only two years before. The Opus 76 are works of triumph; the Opus 77, of reverence. In Opus 76, Haydn shows us everything; in Opus 77, he allows only the essentials. The textures are simple, the moods refined. This is music distilled. They, along with some of Bach's works, are among the few pieces that make me feel for a while, after I have heard them, that there is really nothing else worth listening to.

W. A. Mozart (1756-91)
No. 14, K387, in G major (1782)
No. 15, K421, in D minor (1783)
No. 16, K428, in E flat major (1783)
No 17, K458, in B flat major (1784)
No. 18, K464, in A major (1785)
No. 19, K465, in C major (1785)
No. 20, K499, in D major (1786)
No. 21, K575, in D major (1789)
No. 22, K589, in B flat major (1790)
No. 23, K590, in F major (1790)

Mozart wrote twenty-three quartets, of which the last ten, listed here, are great works. The first six of the ten, Nos. 14-19, comprise the "Haydn Quartets," written in response to the elder composer's Opus 33 and dedicated to him. The next, No. 20, the "Hoffmeister" quartet, stands alone, while the last three, the "King of Prussia" quartets, were, according to tradition, dedicated to Friedrich Wilhelm II, who was a cellist.[86]

The "Haydn" quartets, Nos. 14-19, bring into the quartet, for the first time, the emotional range of opera. Listen to them as an album. The "King of Prussia" Quartets, Nos. 21-23, on the other hand, remind one a little of Haydn's Opus 77, in that they reduce quartet music to its essentials. The gestures are simple, the contemplations profound. Yet even in these lighter-textured pieces, we can hear the emotional ambiguity that is Mozart's signature. We hear sadness and delight, torment and release in quick alternation, and very often at the same time. Mozart surrounded his disappointments with the effervescence of serenade, and it is this more than anything else that attracts to Mozart the first loyalty of so many music-lovers.

Mozart's six string quintets, which are scored for two violas, with cello and two violins, must also be mentioned; they are equal to his quartets. The third and the fourth quintets, *K515 in C major* and *K516 in G minor,* written as a pair in 1787, are Mozart's greatest chamber works. Any exploration of his chamber music should begin with, or culminate with, these two quintets. Fortunately, they are favorites with performers and can be heard often in concert.

Ludwig van Beethoven (1770-1827)
Opus 18, Nos. 1-6, (1798-1800)
Opus 59, Nos. 1-3, the "Razumovsky Quartets" (1806)
Opus 74, the "Harp," in E flat major (1809)
Opus 95, "Serioso," in F minor (1810)
Opus 127, in E flat major (1822-25)
Opus 130, in B flat major (1825-26)
Opus 131, in C sharp minor (1825-26)
Opus 132, in A minor (1825)
Opus 133, the "Grosse Fuge,"
originally the last movement of Opus 130;
Opus 135, in F major (1826)

Beethoven's quartets have inspired many books, both philosophical and technical, and in these modest pages I have already described them in outline (pp. 20-22). Suffice it to say that, like Shakespeare's tragedies in literature, Beethoven's quartets stand alone in music. They are the benchmark.

At first, Beethoven followed the tradition of publishing quartets in albums, but he was ever impatient with convention, and the last eight quartets were published as separate works. Their canvases are too vast to be viewed with companion works.

To my ears, the best introduction to Beethoven's quartets is not the group of early quartets, the six of Opus 18, which are overshadowed by Haydn's Opus 76 and 77. Begin instead with the first of the three Razumovsky Quartets, Opus 59 No. 1, in F major. The cello melody in the first few measures swings open the door to the Romantic century. Once you are hooked by this piece, which charms the heart while it is busy demolishing what music had been before it, turn to its emotional opposite, intense and mysterious, the Opus 59 No. 2, in E minor. Listen your way through the difficult Opus 59 No. 3, in C major, then the delightful "Harp" Quartet, so called because of the pizzicato arpeggios in the first movement, and finally the violent "Serioso." These five are the "middle quartets" and are often recorded together for CD albums.

Listening to the late quartets, like watching Shakespeare's plays, is an undertaking to be resumed at intervals throughout a lifetime. Quartet players and composers still consider these quartets to set the standard for music in the twentieth century — not to speak of the nineteenth. If the late quartets are new to you, begin with the first, the Opus 127. Its opening E-flat chords knock at the door to the soul. Once you have let them in, music can never be the same for you.[87]

Of the other late quartets, the most approachable (and the greatest — Beethoven's *Lear*) is the Opus 131, in C sharp minor. Listen to this one next. It was this piece that taught me to listen to quartets — but I could only start at the pinnacle because I stayed there to listen many times. Still ahead, in order of difficulty, are the great A minor quartet, Opus 132, with its transcendent slow movement; the humorous, squirrely Opus 135, in F major; and — hardest of all to assimilate — the monumental, sprawling Opus 130, in B flat. When you are ready to tackle Opus 130, abandon caution and hear it with its original last movement, the Grosse Fuge, which audiences are still not ready for, 170 years after it was written.

Beethoven also wrote a viola quintet, *Opus 29, in C major (1801)*. It is a lovely piece, undeservedly neglected by performers.

Franz Schubert (1797-1828)
No. 13, D804, in A minor (1824)
No. 14, D810, in D minor "Death and the Maiden" (1824)
No. 15, D887, in G major (1826)

Of Schubert's fifteen quartets, these last three are the masterpieces. No. 14, in D minor, is by far the most often performed - in fact, *too* often; it is one of the very few quartets that has ʳained the status of warhorse. Nevertheless, it is a great work. ..ubert's quartets were the first to build on Beethoven's Romantic foundations, but in one sense they resemble Mozart's: their composer thought primarily in terms of a singable line. The second movement of the "Death and the Maiden" Quartet consists of variations on Schubert's song of that name. The quartet's companion piece, in A minor, is its equal, though it is programmed and recorded much less frequently.

As for the G major Quartet, it is repetitious and vast, like a song with a dozen verses, and it might well be the most difficult of string quartet masterpieces to perform convincingly. It compares with late Beethoven, too, in its challenge to the listener. The only recording I know of that makes it work is by the Quartetto Italiano. Instead of hurrying through it, the Italiano plays it in long breaths, on its own terms.

Schubert wrote two other great works involving violin, viola, and cello: the unforgettable *String Quintet*, for two violins, viola, and two cellos, *D956, in C major*, written in 1828, Schubert's last year, and the scintillating *"Trout" Quintet*, for piano, violin, viola, cello, and double bass, *D667, in A major*, dating from 1819.

2. The National Traditions of the Nineteenth Century

Germany

Felix Mendelssohn (1809-1847)
Opus 44, Nos. 1-3, in D major, E minor, and E flat major (1837-8)
Opus 80, in F minor (1847)

Like Mozart and Schubert, Mendelssohn thought of music above all in terms of melody, and his quartets are graced with soaring songs. For some tastes he is a little schmaltzy, although his best pieces are nonetheless beautiful. The charge that he is superficial, though, is false; he is merely sane. Moreover, his works are a satisfying study for admirers of formal elegance. He published six quartets; the last four are the best. If possible, listen to Opus 44 as an album. Otherwise, choose the second, in E minor. Opus 80, his elegy for his composer-sister, Fanny Mendelssohn-Hensel, is also lovely, and an admirable statement of grieving as experienced by a fundamentally happy man.

When played with the right balance of delicacy and fury, Mendelssohn's sizzling *String Octet*, for four violins, two violas, and two cellos, *Opus 20, in E flat (1825)*, brings audiences to their feet. To write a true full-length eight-voice piece for strings is basically impossible, but Mendelssohn, at sixteen, did not know that. No one else among the great composers has managed it.[88] With it, Mendelssohn became, and still is, the youngest composer to write a work that remains in the classical repertoire.

Robert Schumann (1810-1856)
Opus 41, Nos. 1-3, in A minor, F major, and A major (1842)

Of Schumann's three quartets, the third, in A major, is the best — a must for Schumann lovers. Like much of his other work, the quartets are episodic and pianistic; they sound like they were written for four hands on the keyboard rather than four bows on the strings. The chamber works for piano and strings that followed in the same year — the *Piano Quartet, Opus 47 in E flat major,* and the *Piano Quintet, Opus 44, in E flat major* — build on the string quartets and are, deservedly, heard more often.

Johannes Brahms (1833-97)
Opus 51, No. 1, in C minor (1859, revised 1873)
Opus 51, No. 2, in A minor (1859, revised 1873)
Opus 67, in B flat major (1875)

Brahms had a knack of reaching out with a long-limbed melody and hauling the listener by the ear down into emotional seas. A mere two measures have gone by and we are immersed. Many listeners have noticed the heavy orchestral texture of his three quartets, but Brahms manages to turn weight into power.

The first and third of the quartets are great Brahms, the one stormy, the other as sunny as this composer's North Sea weather permits. The second quartet, Opus 51, No. 2, though, is one of his lesser efforts.

The Russians

Alexander Borodin (1833-87)
Quartet No. 2, in D major (1881-87)

Of this lovely piece I have already written in these pages. Borodin's first quartet, in A major (1877-79), is not a match for the second.

Pyotr Tchaikovsky (1840-93)
Opus 11, in D major (1871)
Opus 22, in F major (1874)
Opus 30, in E flat minor (1876)

The Russian ensembles that are now touring and recording frequently in the West have at last made it possible to hear Tchaikosky's three quartets. All are superb, but are neglected by Western performers, audiences, critics, and recording companies. Tchaikovsky, who was a Mozart fan, used the formal discipline of chamber music to contain the sprawling emotions of his larger works, and the sentimentality of the concertos and symphonies is therefore elevated to tragedy. The quartets are notable for their use of folk dances — for example, the 7/4 pulse (actually two measures of 6/8 alternating with one of 9/8) in the wonderful slow movement of the second quartet, Opus 22. The quartets are elegantly written: don't be surprised to hear a fugue (Tchaikovsky? a fugue?) in the second quartet's last movement. The sweet melodies of Opus 11 and the monumental chordal slow movement of Opus 30 are not to be missed; however, Opus 22 is the masterpiece.

More frequently heard is Tchaikovsky's *String Sextet, "Souvenir de Florence," Opus 70 (1887-90, revised 1891-92).* This, too, is a marvelous piece.

The Bohemians

Bedrich Smetana (1824-84)
No. 1, "From my Life," in E minor (1876)

This autobiographical quartet, written as the composer was going deaf, is dramatic and touching, especially in live performance.

Antonín Dvořák (1841-1904)
Opus 51, in E flat major (1878-79)
Opus 61, in C major (1881)
Opus 96, "American," in F major (1893)
Opus 105, in A flat major (1895)
Opus 106, in G major (1895)

Of Dvořák's fourteen quartets, these last five comprise one of the finest quartet cycles of the nineteenth century.

The composer spent his early career as an orchestral violist, and his skill in string-writing has no peer. Not even Mozart matched Dvořák's ability to make the string quartet sound gorgeous. No one else has given the viola such prominence, either; in these quartets, the viola, instead of the cello, takes the role of secondary melodist after the first violin. Like Schubert, Dvořák was above all a writer of melodies; after listening, expect to have some trouble getting these tunes out of your head.

Three of Dvořák's last five quartets, Opus 51, 96, and 106, are graced with Bohemian folk melodies. (Opus 96, the "American," was written during a three-year stay in the United States, but its pentatonic tunes are Czech.) Opus 96 has become something of a warhorse. All five are equally beautiful.

Other National Schools

Good quartets were written in France, England, Scandinavia, and Italy during the Romantic period. Their composers are not among my own favorites, but I list them here for those who enjoy the composers' other works. If you like the symphonies, operas, or oratorios, you'll no doubt like the quartets.

Giuseppe Verdi (1813-1901)
String Quartet in E minor (1873)

César Franck (1822-1890)
String Quartet in D major (1889)

Edvard Grieg (1843-1907)
Opus 27, in G minor (1877-78)

Edward Elgar (1857-1934)
Opus 83, in E minor (1918)

Giacomo Puccini (1858-1924)
"Crisantemi" (1890)

3. The Modern Period: Modal Nationalists

For the sake of clarity, we can organize the great quartet composers of the modern period into two groups: those who continued the national schools of the previous century, often reaching into folk music to take up Debussy's experiments in modal scales; and those who extended the nineteenth-century German experiments in chromaticism to their logical conclusion in atonalism. But the two paths cross, and many composers tried out both of them.

Claude Debussy (1862-1918)
String Quartet, Opus 10 (1893)

For quartets, the twentieth century begins in 1893, with Debussy. In this masterpiece, the great French innovator imported into the sanctum of the quartet the experiments in tonality and harmony that he was carrying out in his vocal and orchestral works. In Germany, composers were pushing traditional harmony into a tortured chromaticism in order to find a way out of the limits of key relations. It took a Parisian to find an elegant solution: instead of abandoning harmony, he took leave of the major and minor scales. He wrote modal and whole-tone melodies, and, as a result, harmonies are set pleasantly adrift.

Unlike most of his other pieces, Debussy's string quartet is in the traditional four movements, and it is the only piece to which he gave the traditional opus number. The composer seemed to be signaling his conscious intention to wrench the quartet out of the hands of the nineteenth century and to demonstrate that even this musical icon could be reforged into a modern shape. Begin your exploration of twentieth-century quartets with this piece.

Leos Janácek (1854-1928)
No. 1 "Kreutzer Sonata" (1923)
No. 2 "Intimate Letters" (1928)

Like his countryman Smetana, the Czech composer Leos Janácek wrote autobiographical quartets. Both these pieces expressed his autumnal, unfulfilled love for another man's wife.

As befitting the quartets of a great opera composer, Janácek's string voices seem to be conversing throughout. These beautiful works present Romantic storytelling in twentieth-century sound. Fortunately, now that Czech ensembles are bringing their great quartet tradition to Western audiences, Janácek's masterpieces have caught on among North American performers and are programmed fairly often.

Béla Bartók (1881-1945)
No. 1, Opus 7 (1908)
No. 2, Opus 17 (1915-17)
No. 3 (1927)
No. 4 (1928)
No. 5 (1934)
No. 6 (1939)

The Hungarian composer Béla Bartók wrote six quartets, and he was planning another when he died. Many performers and listeners place the Bartók cycle second in greatness only to Beethoven's. I myself would place Haydn's and Shostakovich's quartets before Bartók's — but not by much. The six quartets span Bartók's life and should be listened to in sequence.

Already in the first of these, Bartók continues Debussy's experiments in tonality by writing melodies outside the major and minor modes. The composer was a pioneering ethnomusicologist, and he brought back from his excursions among Magyar peasants not only folk modes but the use of drones to establish the modal home-note, and, also, the driving rhythms that make all his music as thrilling as Haydn's.

Like Beethoven in his last quartets, Bartók broke open the quartet's traditional four-movement box and cast his quartets in a variety of molds. He carried much further the experiments in string sound that Beethoven initiated — creating, for example, the mysterious, squeaky "night music" that first appears in the second quartet.

As in Shostakovich's fifteen quartets, one can hear in Bartók's six an emotional record of the first half of our century — of its violent despairs and its wild sorrows. Listen to these stunning

156

pieces at night, in a quiet place, when you are ready for an earful of plain speaking. Of the six, the fifth is the masterpiece.

Dmitri Shostakovich (1906-75)

No. 1, Op. 49, in C major (1938)
No. 2, Op. 68, in A major (1944)
No. 3, Op. 73, in F major (1946)
No. 4, Op. 83, in D major (1949)
No. 5, Op. 92, in B flat major (1953)
No. 6, Op. 101, in G major (1956)
No. 7, Op. 108, in F sharp minor (1960)
No. 8, Op. 110, in C minor (1960)
No. 9, Op. 117, in E flat major (1964)
No. 10, Op. 118, in A flat major (1964)
No. 11, Op. 122, in F minor (1966)
No. 12, Op. 133, in D flat major (1968)
No. 13, Op. 138, in B flat minor (1970)
No. 14, Op. 142, in F sharp major (1972-73)
No. 15, Op. 144, in E flat minor (1974)

A brief portrait of Shostakovich as a quartet composer, along with an appreciation of his great Third Quartet, is given in the second appendix to this book. A proper appreciation of his fifteen quartets would take an entire volume. Into these private pieces, Shostakovich felt free to pour out the expressions of a musical mastery that has had no equal since Beethoven. Like Beethoven, he preserved the truth of an epoch — of its aesthetic perceptions, its emotional depths, and its social and political history. He is the pre-eminent quartet composer of our century. One of the many happy results of the collapse of the Soviet tyranny has been the release of this composer's work from its prison of obscurity and misrepresentation. Much credit for this belongs to the Borodin String Quartet, which has frequently performed the full quartet cycle in North America.

The fifteen quartets can be divided into four groups. In the first two, the composer is learning his craft. The first is quite simple, and both are conservative compared to the rest. (Like Beethoven, Shostakovich waited till his thirties to tackle quartet writing.) The third through the tenth quartets, comprising the middle group, are masterpieces. They display, each differently, all the composer's gifts: for melody, for thrilling sounds, for tragic storytelling, for bitter social comment, for technical virtuosity, for devastating emotional journeys. Like Beethoven's middle and late quartets, these pieces can be listened to again and again without satiety. They are inexhaustible.

The third group, the eleventh through the fourteenth, replace the tragedies of the earlier group with statements of despair. The musical language sometimes approaches atonality, the dissonances are brutal. This is challenging work for the listener.

The fifteenth returns to straightforward tonality and thus is as easily approachable as the middle quartets. But it does not sound like they do. Its textures are bare, full of silences in one or another of the instruments; its mood is grief. The piece is unique in the quartet repertoire in consisting of five slow movements. The dark key, E flat minor, one of the most awkward of keys for string players, was perhaps chosen in honor of Tchaikovsky's last quartet in the same key. Both quartets seem to mourn the tragedies of their composers' own lives, and, for the listener, to commemorate the ineluctable sorrows of the human condition.

Also important is Shostakovich's *Piano Quintet* (for string quartet and piano), *Opus 57, in G minor (1940)*. It has long been rather popular with Western audiences, in part for its relatively light-hearted moods.

Samuel Barber (1910-1981)
String Quartet, Opus 11 (1936)

This American composer's sole quartet is not to be missed. It is best known through the "Adagio for Strings," an arrangement of the quartet's chordal slow movement that the composer made for orchestra at the behest of Arturo Toscanini. (Barber also arranged the movement for a cappella choir.) It is harder to play the adagio as a string quartet; the intensity of the music, when distilled back down to the original four voices, is almost beyond bearing. When played right, it can reduce an audience to tears.

Barber draws on the Romanticism of nineteenth century Germany, rather than on anything originally American. His outright emotionalism and conservative harmonies earned him the scorn of modernist critics and performers. He was considered behind his times. The advent of post-modernism has now shown otherwise: he was ahead.

Benjamin Britten (1913-1976)
No. 1 (1941)
No. 2 (1945)
No. 3 (1975)

England's greatest composer wrote three great quartets. Like his friend Shostakovich, Britten was a melodist, a virtuoso in compositional technique, and a pioneer in soundmaking. Without straying far from the major and minor scales, the mesmerizing sound of these quartets seems to emerge from a lost tradition — unless their precedent be the reverberations of voices in the vaults of English cathedrals. Most remarkable of the three works is the second, with its monumental last movement, a set of twenty-one variations on a short, arresting theme.

I would place the following composers in the second rank of the quartet writers who carried national traditions into the twentieth century.

Charles Ives (1874-1954)
String Quartet No. 1 "A Revival Service (1896)
String Quartet No. 2 (1907-13)

The American composer Charles Ives' first quartet is a compendium of American folk songs, the second an essay in his characteristic polytonality. The two pieces are, understandably, championed by American performers, but I cannot say I like the music much.

Maurice Ravel (1875-1937)
String Quartet in F (1902-03)

This is one of the few quartets that is performed more often than it deserves. It is a lovely homage to Debussy, but without the greatness of its model.

Igor Stravinsky (1882-1971)
Three Pieces for String Quartet (1914)

Despite his periods of neo-classicism, Stravinsky did not attempt a full string quartet. He wrote only occasional short works in the medium, and, one of them, the set of "Three Pieces," is sometimes encountered in the concert hall and on recordings. It is vintage Stravinsky: iconoclastic, theatrical, sometimes humorous, and fiercely rhythmic.

Heitor Villa-Lobos (1887-1959)
Quartets Nos. 1-17 (1915-57)

The seventeen quartets written over forty-two years by the great Brazilian composer combined modal modernism with folk melodies and rhythms. They are only recently gaining much attention from North American performers and listeners. The young Mexican ensemble Cuarteto Latinoamericano, for example, is now recording the cycle.

Sergey Prokofiev (1891-1953)
Opus 50 (1930)
Opus 92 (1942)

Prokofiev's two quartets show the influence of both the French and the Russian traditions. They skimp disappointingly on the exhilarating wildness of his piano works, but they are delightful nevertheless. The second, with its Tatar folk elements, is the better piece.

Paul Hindemith (1895-1963)
No. 1, Op. 10 (1918)
No. 2, Op. 16 (1920)
No. 3, Op. 22 (1921)
No. 4, Op. 32 (1923)
No. 5 (1943)
No. 6 (1945)

The German-born Hindemith (who emigrated in 1940 to Switzerland and the United States) was a professional quartet player, both as a violist and second violinist, and also a neo-classical theorist. Only some of his music deserves its reputation for a too-cold formalism. The third quartet, which combines elegant string-writing and late-Romantic chromaticism, is a beautiful piece.

William Walton (1902-83)
String Quartet (1946-47)

This English composer's quartet, in which the influence of Debussy can be heard clearly, is a lovely piece which deserves more frequent performance.

Other twentieth-century nationalists are:

Gabriel Fauré, French (1845-1924)
Opus 121 in E minor (1923-24)

Jean Sibelius, Finnish (1865-1957)
Opus 56, in D minor, "Voces Intimae" (1908-09)

Ralph Vaughan Williams, English (1872-1958)
No. 2 in A minor (1942-44)

Ernest Bloch, Swiss (1880-1959)
String Quartets Nos. 2-5 (1946-56)

Darius Milhaud, French (1892-1974)
String Quartets Nos. 1-18 (1912-62)

Michael Tippett, English (b. 1905)
String Quartets Nos. 1-5 (1934-92)

Alberto Ginastera, Argentinean (1916-83)
No. 1 (1948)
No. 2 (1958)
No. 3, with soprano voice (1973)

4. The Modern Period: The Second Viennese School and its Followers

Arnold Schoenberg (1874-1951)
No. 1, Op. 7, in D minor (1905)
No. 2, Op. 2, in F sharp minor (1907-08)
No. 3, Op. 30 (1927)
No. 4. Op. 37 (1936)

Most classical audiences have heard that Arnold Schoenberg was the inventor of atonal music and the leading apostle of musical modernism, but rather few people have actually heard his music. Schoenberg's reputation has made them afraid to listen to him, and, as a result, presenters and performers are for the most part afraid to program him. Nevertheless he was one of the greatest of composers, as his four numbered quartets attest.

Listened to in sequence, these quartets unfold Schoenberg's journey from Romanticism into modernism. The extremes of chromaticism characterize the first quartet. By the final movement of the second quartet, Schoenberg has almost entirely committed himself to the logical step of treating all twelve tones of the chromatic scale equally. No note stands as the tonic, and there are no more keys. This is atonalism. Musical reality has been reconstructed; Romanticism has become Expressionism. Schoenberg added a soprano to the second quartet's last two movements (thus the work is really a quintet); the singer's angular, homeless melodies define the sound of angst.

The third and fourth quartets are entirely atonal, but, in mood, less unsettling than the second. Because Schoenberg does not abandon traditional rhythms, the emotional content of the pieces remains accessible, despite the lack of harmony and key, and despite the resulting rootlessness of the melodies. Both pieces are approachable, likable, and beautiful — not at all scary. Once you elbow your way past their formidable reputation, you will find great music.

Early in his career Schoenberg wrote one of the outstanding chamber works of the late Romantic period: *"Verklärte Nacht"* *(Transfigured Night), Op. 4 (1899)*, for string sextet. Together with Tchaikovsky's "Souvenir de Florence," it is one of the two finest sextet in the repertoire.

Alban Berg (1885-1935)
Opus 3 (1910)
"Lyric Suite" (1925-26)

Two of Schoenberg's senior pupils, Berg and Anton Webern, were great composers, and the three composers together are often said to comprise the "Second Viennese School" (with Haydn, Mozart, Beethoven, and Schubert composing the first). Berg's two quartets are probably performed more frequently than any other atonal work for string quartet, and with good reason. More so than any other composer, including his teacher, Berg managed to employ atonalism as a medium for emotional expressiveness. The "Lyric Suite" is an encrypted love letter. If you are one of the many listeners who have never been able to stand atonal music for more than a minute or two, try this fine piece.

Anton Webern (1883-1945)
Five Movements, Op. 5, 1909
Six Bagatelles, Op. 9, 1913
String Quartet, Op. 28, 1936-38

Webern's expressionist miniatures are rather strange, but lovely.

I will not attempt to list here a selection of the many works for string quartet that have been written in an atonal style. Few have managed to enter the permanent concert repertoire, and it is hard to say which will ever do so; my own guess would be, "Not many." The works of one great American composer, however, belong in any history of the string quartet.

Elliott Carter (b. 1908)
No. 1 (1951)
No. 2 (1958-59)
No. 3 (1971)
No. 4 (1986)

In his quartets, Carter deconstructs not only melody and harmony, but also rhythm. That is to say, the listener cannot identify a tune, a key, or a beat. With the composers of the Second Viennese School, there is always a sense of rhythm, even when melody and harmony seem absent, and so the music can still express feeling. But Carter's quartets are, to my ears, pure abstractions; they are music divorced from its roots in emotion. Listening to them is rather like visiting an exhibit of the geo-

163

metric paintings of Piet Mondrian. Both artists are interesting, challenging, and in their aesthetic integrity and virtuosity altogether admirable, but the works lack the means to convey warmth or to inspire it.

Carter is comparable to Bach, it seems to me, in that — just as Bach brought Baroque music to perfection after the Baroque period had ended and younger musicians had moved onward — Carter has brought modernism to its logical conclusion while postmodern aesthetics have already begun to flourish all around him.

5. Post-Modern Quartets

Guiding a listener through the vital profusion of contemporary quartet-writing is rather like guiding a group of hikers through a redwood forest: the way is so open that any path is likely to be as valid as another, and, looking up from the ground, it is impossible to tell which are the tallest trees. I can do no more than guess which post-modern quartets will last into the next century, and the only way to guess is to say which I like.

For post-modern quartets — most of them written after 1970 — composers seem to be taking one of two paths: syncretism or revisionism. Both paths aim toward the audience. All these composers want to repair the breakdown in communication between classical musicians and their audience that was occasioned by the uncompromising difficulties of modernist music.

What distinguishes the syncretists is their attempt, in one way or another, to combine the various discoveries of modernism with the communicative power of Romanticism. They want the classical audience back, but at the same time they don't want to abandon all of modernism's aesthetic advances. They are unwilling to return to the straightforward scales, keys, and harmonies of the eighteenth and nineteenth centuries, but in other ways they have embraced the Romantic aesthetic — its direct appeals to emotion, its story-telling, its dramatic journeys, its philosophical meditations.

A second group of post-modern composers is made up of revisionists. To them, modernism has reached a dead end, and the only way for music to find its bearings again is to start over. These composers have turned to the musics of much earlier times — including the traditional musics of Asia. They have also embraced popular music and jazz. In this group are minimalists, composers in the world music movement, jazz and pop crossover composers, neo-romantics, and neo-medievalists.

Post-Modern Syncretists

R. Murray Schafer (Canadian, b. 1933)
No. 1 (1970)
No. 2 "Waves" (1976)
No. 3 (1981)
No. 4, with soprano voice (1988-89)
No. 5, "Rosalind" (1989)
No. 6, "Part Wild Horse's Mane" (1994)

Perhaps the most distinguished quartet-writer among the post-modern syncretists is the Canadian Murray Schafer. His first five quartets have been recorded by the Orford Quartet,[89] and anyone curious to explore post-modern syncretism might begin there. Much of Schafer's work in other media combines opera, theater, and performance art, and, similarly, his sixth quartet, as yet unrecorded, accompanies a Tai Qi set. An appreciation of Schafer's work and of his Quartet No. 1 is given in this book as Appendix B.

Other syncretists whose quartets I like include the Canadian composer Sydney Hodkinson, the American composers Martin Bresnick and Robert Greenberg, the Polish composer Henryk Gorecki, and the Australian composer Peter Sculthorpe. No doubt there are many others whose music I will like when I hear it.

Post-Modern Revisionists

Terry Riley (American, b. 1935)
"Cadenza on the Night Plain" (1984)
"Salome Dances for Peace" (1985-86)

165

Riley's stunning "Cadenza" and monumental "Salome" are, in my opinion, as good as anything written for string quartet since the death of Shostakovich. They are as dramatic and moving, as full of beautiful sounds and melodies, as the best quartets of the nineteenth-century national schools, without resembling them at all.

Riley spent ten years in India studying with the Hindustani master Pandit Pran Nath. As a performer, he improvises on saxophone and keyboard. Jazz, Indian music, and story-telling based on Native American myths inform his compositions. As did the composers of the Middle Ages, he sees music primarily as a medium for spiritual awakening. In his words: "The purpose of music is to bring people to a heightened state of awareness."[90]

His radical revisionism has not endeared him to critics and to most performers, who — unfortunately for listeners — continue to ignore him. However, my best guess is that, when the dust has settled, he will be included among the great quartet composers.

Riley is sometimes credited as the initiator of minimalism, but he does not consider himself a minimalist. He does not use the radical harmonic simplicity and the static pacing of two better known American minimalists:

Philip Glass (American, b. 1937)
No. 3 "Mishima" (1985)
No. 4 "Buczal" (1990)
No. 5 (1991)

Many listeners find Glass's early works tediously repetitive, but his later works, including these beautiful quartets, are much more complex and dramatic.

Steve Reich (American, b. 1936)
"Different Trains"

This remarkable work, for string quartet, pre-recorded train-whistles, and fragments of spoken voice, evokes memories of American passenger trains in contrast with recollections of the trains that transported victims of the Holocaust. It is a superb example of quartet story-telling and of the collaboration of electronic and acoustic instruments.

The works of Riley, Glass, and Reich have helped establish the first true American quartet style. These composers' interest in clear tonality, repetitive figures, dance-rhythms, and religious themes is echoed in the neo-medievalism of such European composers as the Estonian Arvo Pärt and the Englishman John Tavener, both of whom have written beautiful quartets.

6. Twenty Best of the Best

The foregoing list of great quartets is a long one. The following summary is offered for listeners who want more guidance and fewer choices in getting started with quartet listening. The summary below includes representative great quartets from each historical period. All the works listed are available on recordings.

1. Josef Haydn, *Opus 77, No.1*
Alternate: Any one of the six quartets of Opus 76

2. W.A. Mozart, *String Quartet No. 15, in D minor*
Alternate: No. 19, in C major

3. Ludwig van Beethoven, *Opus 59, No. 1*
Alternate: Opus 59, No. 2

4. Ludwig van Beethoven, *Opus 127*
Alternate: Opus 131

5. Franz Schubert, *No. 14, "Death and the Maiden"*

6. Johannes Brahms, *Opus 51, No. 1*

7. Pyotr Tchaikovsky, *Opus 22*

8. Alexander Borodin, *String Quartet No. 2*

9. Antonín Dvořák, *Opus 106*
Alternate: Opus 96, "American"

10. Claude Debussy, *Opus 10*

11. Leos Janácek, *String Quartet No. 2*
Alternate: No. 1

12. Samuel Barber, *Opus 11*

13. Béla Bartók, *String Quartet No. 5*
Alternate: No. 6

14. Arnold Schoenberg, *String Quartet No. 4*
Alternate: No. 3

15. Alban Berg, *"Lyric Suite"*

16. Benjamin Britten, *String Quartet No. 2*

17. Dmitri Shostakovich, *String Quartet No. 3*
Alternate: No. 8

18. Dmitri Shostakovich, *String Quartet No. 15*

19. R. Murray Schafer, *any of Nos. 1-5*

20. Terry Riley, *"Cadenza on the Night Plain."*

Appendix B

1. The Village of Mankind

Dmitri Shostakovich's Quartet No. 3 (1946)

Shostakovich was the most cinematic of all the great composers. He wrote film scores for a living and for political cover, but almost all of his music shows the influence of film. While many composers have imitated the inflections of the human voice to communicate emotion through instrumental music, Shostakovich's melodies imitate physical gestures. Once the listener's imagination is attuned to this, entire works can seem like a progression of portraits of people in motion as the composer unreels a filmscript in sound.

In writing cinematic music, Shostakovich was in one sense conforming to his times — but not with the slavishness that many Westerners have accused him of. Programmatic music — music that tells a story — was required of all Soviet composers, in accordance with the doctrine of Socialist Realism. Under Stalin and his successors, works of art were expected to praise the idealized heroic worker and to inspire commitment to the perfected communist society of the future. No one understands better than the tyrant what power art has to unite people in an opinion or a mood, and Stalin, in particular, intended to harness that power in support of his regime. As the Soviet Union's leading composer, therefore, Shostakovich endured constant and direct scrutiny from Stalin himself. The composer's music was carefully vetted for the loyalty of its implied stories. The zealous but obtuse persecutions of official censorship dogged him throughout his adult life, which was spent entirely under Communism (he was born in 1906 and died in 1975).

During his lifetime, most Western critics and audiences, and many Western performers as well, considered Shostakovich to be, at worst, Stalin's musical toady, or, at best, an unwilling but terrorized apologist. An opposite picture — of a wily, sarcastic dissident — appears in the composer's tape-recorded memoir, *Testimony*, which was smuggled out of Russia and published in the West in 1979.[91] But the book was discredited and its compiler, Solomon Volkov, denounced as a fabricator. Since the fall of Communism, however, the picture presented in *Testimony* has been shown to be the true one.[92]

Shostakovich's great purpose as an artist was just as he said it was in his memoir: to bear witness to the sufferings of the Soviet people under the Stalinist tyranny. Almost all of his mature compositions are veiled statements of political protest. Required by official doctrine to write programmatic music, he stood the doctrine on its head. He wrote to the wrong program. For the optimistic falsehood of Socialist Realism, he substituted an angry, grieving truth. He wrenched the tool of music out of the censors' hands and turned it into a weapon of defiance. His music parodies official bombast, sneers at the political police, paints terrifying portraits of persecution, and mourns for the murdered and for the bereft. Often he expressed his purpose too unmistakably to fool anyone except Westerners. For this boldness he was periodically silenced.

Many of the composer's colleagues and friends were imprisoned or murdered for un-Socialist realism in art, but Shosta–kovich was a survivor. Commanded to lie in his music, he lied instead with words. He deceitfully announced Socialist Realist programs intended to divert censors from noticing the anti-Realism actually expressed by the music. Or, similarly, he accepted the misleading titles suggested by the authorities. In the West, the best known example is the Fifth Symphony, which the composer wrote in 1937, after one of his public disgraces during the most severe period of the Stalinist terror. Shostakovich disingenuously presented his new symphony as a statement of repentance and submission — although in fact it was yet another statement of protest. The famous title, "A Soviet Artist's Creative Reply to Just Criticism," was not his. It was forced on him as a condition of the censors' approval of the premiere. The music itself has nothing to do with the title.[93]

Several of Shostakovich's symphonies were banned, and as for operas, whose stories cannot be veiled, he had to cease writing them. Partly as a result, he found a haven in string quartets. The subtlety of the quartet form, and its tradition of performance before small, sophisticated audiences, made quartet-writing relatively safe. The music was less likely to be recognized as a challenge to the regime. In the quartets, Shostakovich felt able to speak frankly without much fear of reprisal — although he did not hesitate to protect the pieces with misleading titles and ambiguous program notes. Only the Fourth Quartet, which defied official anti-Semitism with melodies openly based in Jewish folk music, was banned.[94]

Because the Shostakovich quartets are relatively frank and transparent, they are easier for the Western listener to understand than the symphonies are. The composer's symphonic parodies of official bombast may sound, to our ears, merely as bombast. But even if we know nothing of the quartets' programs — and here the scholarly disquisitions on form and technique in CD booklets are of no help — it would be hard to mistake them for anything but tragic stories.

Of Shostakovich's fifteen quartets, the Third, in F major, is perhaps the greatest. It was the only music the composer wrote during the year 1946. He described it as "a war quartet," and as such it belongs among several works written during the 1940's, and later as well, which the composer disguised by plausibly pretending that their subject was Hitler's war. The "Leningrad Symphony" (the Ninth, written in 1945), and "To the Memory of Victims of Fascism" (the Eighth Quartet, written in 1960), for example, are smokescreen titles familiar to Western listeners. The real villains in all these musical dramas were Stalin and Stalinism. The composer said in *Testimony:*

> I feel eternal pain for those who were killed by Hitler, but I feel no less pain for those killed on Stalin's orders. I suffer for everyone who was

tortured, shot or starved to death. There were millions of them in our country before the war with Hitler began. The war brought much new sorrow and much new destruction, but I haven't forgotten the terrible prewar years. That is what all my symphonies, beginning with the Fourth, are all about, including the Seventh and the Eighth.[95]

When Shostakovich called his Third Quartet a war quartet, then, the war he was referring to was the Soviet Union's war against its own people. For the premiere of the quartet in Moscow in December, 1946, he provided this guardedly worded description of the five movements:

1. Calm unawareness of the future cataclysm.
2. Rumblings of unrest and anticipation.
3. The forces of war unleashed.
4. Homage to the dead.
5. The eternal question: Why? And for what?[96]

Members of the Lafayette Quartet, after recording the piece for the Dorian label in 1994, expanded on the composer's summary:

Sharon: The first movement is the day before the disaster under the Soviet regime, the last happy day, when things were fine and dandy, or at least seemed like they were. And in the second movement, clouds are forming, the tanks are closing in. Third movement–

Ann: The boots.

Pam: The triumph of evil.

Sharon: Evil takes over. The fourth is the funeral march, and the fifth is Shostakovich's –

Pam: Philosophical epilogue. His personal assessment.

Ann: The piece ends with you wondering if the world's even going to continue.

Pam: I personally think, just to add to that, in the last movement, when it comes to the Jewish theme, or the one that seems like a Jewish theme, it's speaking of those who at the time said that we're all Jews and we're all being treated as the scapegoats of society. It's known that Shostakovich had that view, and that's why you can't play that movement without a heavy heart. It's such a powerful piece. All of his quartets are. They're monuments. For me, playing the piece is like listening to Bach's Goldberg Variations. You're changed by the time you've gone through the process. You've experienced a lifetime.

To my ears, the filmscript of Shostakovich's Third Quartet recounts the sacking of a village. The invading soldiers are the villagers' own countrymen. Shostakovich himself was a city-dweller, and what he feared and witnessed were invasions by secret police. But a musical cinematographer must make use of the folk music of the countryside. The dance tunes, love songs, and dirges of the Russian peasantry are never far from the surface of Shostakovich's music. In the first of the five movements of the Third Quartet, then, the scene, as I hear it, is a village street. The opening melody in the first violin portrays a child skipping down the roadway. The tune is playful but erratic, as if the child keeps stopping for a moment when she senses hostile eyes. The second theme — the movement is in sonata form — interrupts quietly and ominously.

The quartet's second movement brings the adults into the street. It begins with a plodding, repetitive one-two-three minor triad, E, G, B, sounded in the viola — one of the composer's somber, thumping peasant dances. After two measures, the first violin joins in with a jagged, rollicking melody that infects the dance with anxiety and alarm. Eventually the music subsides into a series of staccato, pianissimo chords, which bring to mind the image of a frightened group of people walking about on tiptoe, as if the peasants are hoping that their village will somehow be overlooked. The movement ends on an unsettling bitonal chord, as the upper three instruments subside into C minor while the cello comes to rest on a double-stop in E minor. The cello's bass E-natural grates pianissimo against the first violin's E-flat.

Bitonality — writing in two keys at once — is a hallmark of Shostakovich's sound. Often in his music, some instruments play in one key while others insist on another key, so that two sets of harmonies are heard simultaneously. His melodies, too, tend to slip from one key to another and back again; here the bitonality is sequential rather than simultaneous. Sometimes the effect is contentiousness or outright battle; at other moments, there is a profound sense of dislocation and anxiety. Bitonal writing allowed Shostakovich to exercise his great gift for melody, but at the same time to numb the melodies' emotional content. When a tune's harmony is distorted or contradicted, it loses its security and its center. And it was the emotional center of traditional Russian life, above all, that Communism destroyed.

The Third Quartet's third movement opens with a series of fortissimo, double-stopped chords in the three lower instruments — what Ann called "the boots." The village is being stormed. A panicked violin melody soon escalates to a high D, then reverses into a scurrying downward cry, as of civilians fleeing in terror. Then, at intervals throughout the movement, the tramping soldiers in the lower strings pursue the citizens in the upper strings. At one point, a wailing theme in the two violins, reminiscent of Jewish folk music, is accompanied by an ominous muttering of diminished fifths in the viola and cello, as if the soldiers are loitering in the background while the villagers emerge from their homes to discover their dead in the street. Soon afterward, a viola solo rollicks like an officer swaggering across the village square, with his troops strutting about him in a pizzicato accompaniment.

As the third movement closes, Shostakovich recapitulates each of its scenes. The opening melody of alarm and flight returns, now played in a hushed terror. Then the village women wail in the violins; the officer swaggers; the soldiers' boots stomp on all sixteen strings — all four instruments played fortissimo with quadruple stops. Finally, the flight melody erupts again, with the viola high on its A string overlapping the first violin in rapid descents, as if a panicked crowd is trampling itself. There is a shriek in the first violin, a thudding of gunfire from all four instruments, and three final stompings as in evil triumph.

The first three movements have played; the booted soldiers have departed. Now the fourth movement begins — a funeral march. Octaves in the lower strings state it first: a slow dirge.

The tune keeps halting irregularly before pushing on, as if the marchers have hardly the strength to carry their dead to their graves. After the first note, the melody stumbles into the next-lower key before regaining its footing. Soon the first violin answers the other instruments with a sighing solo expressive of a sorrow too heavy to be released in tears.

This is not a funeral held in honor of the heroic sacrifices that secured a national victory, as Shostakovich pretended for the program printed for the premiere. It is a procession in stunned and bitter grief for meaningless losses suffered in defeat. The movement is a passacaglia — a form built upon repetition of a melody or a bass line — and Shostakovich's dirge is reiterated seven times, always in the same key of C-sharp minor. The previous three movements have been full of dramatic motion, but in defeat, everything repeats itself deadeningly. Suddenly, when it is stated for the fifth time, the melody accelerates, as if the mourners in sudden horror are hurrying their dead into the graves. They pause for a moment in agony, and then as the melody re-accelerates they flee from the cemetery. Finally, again as a dirge, the melody sounds in the viola as the mourners trudge slowly home. The violins are silent, and the cello alone in accompaniment mutters the rhythm of the marchers' shuffling steps. The effort of burial has left them numb. Everything is lost, and there seems hardly any point in even moving any more.

Yet those who have been spared must continue to live. Somehow they must find a way to grieve, even though the losses have been without meaning. The quartet must therefore have a fifth movement. It begins with a soft waltz tune in the bass of the cello, rollicking, whispery and angular, soon to be joined by a whirling accompaniment in the viola. It is a dance of skeletons. The composer seems to be watching the dance in his thoughts, as he remembers Stalin's Terror, recalling everything, refusing to accept, yet longing for the release of grief.

For the second theme of the last movement, a sorrowing survivor is heard in a keening lament on the first violin. Next, the opening skeleton-dance returns; then, surprisingly, but realistically, too, a sweetly simple nursery-tune appears as the third theme. It is the child of the first movement, stepping back into the street in the same skipping rhythm, first tentatively half-hidden in the cello, then more confident in the first violin.

But the past cannot be erased. The dance of the dead insists on returning — the movement is a sonata-rondo, a form which brings the first theme back after each episode. It is as if the composer cannot keep the memory of his losses from crowding his thoughts. All at once, the funeral march of the previous movement bursts upon the ear. It is played in canon in the viola and cello, while the angry double-stopped violins send up an almost unbearable fortissimo wail. Finally, the memory of the burial subsides in exhaustion on a single note in the cello; the music seems almost to stop.

Then the child's theme returns, this time in the minor, in the muted first violin. The child is playing again, but now her face is covered with tears. Hearing her, seeing her in the imagination, it seems possible at last for the composer and his audience to weep. Soon the second theme of lament returns, and then the skeleton's dance for the last time, fragmented, half-heard among the mists of a muted F-major chord. Slowly the dance dissipates, in a scarcely heard pianissimo. The music surrenders its ghosts to the grave, as the composer, having opened his heart at last, lets go of his dead.

As we listen to Shostakovich's Third Quartet, we can, of course, imagine a succession of scenes different from the ones I have imagined, or indeed no scenes at all. Music grants us that liberty. It is a liberty that recordings, especially, encourage us to take. With repeated hearings, the contours of a piece of music and the voice of a composer become as familiar as the sound and the phrases of a poet whose works we have read many times. Still, not every music-lover finds visual analogs illuminating, as I do. What counts is that the voices of the music, heard between the earphones in the intimate theater of the mind, bind us in sympathy and understanding to the emotions expressed in the sound. Then the unifying magnetism of music joins the solitary listener, in his imagination, to the composer, to the performers, and to other listeners. The scattered community of music-lovers is assembled, and Shostakovich's story, distant in space and time, is made present. It a Russian story, recounting a terrible past about which we Westerners still know very little; and we attend to it like guests at a country funeral where the mourners are a family we barely know. Listening in sympathy, standing near the back of the marching line of mourners, we come to understand that the dead of the Third Quartet are no different from our dead. This sorrow is ours. This village is no single spot on the earth, but the village of mankind.

2. The Music of the Environment:

R. Murray Schafer's Quartet No. 1 (1970)

Before a sold-out recital hall at the University of Victoria School of Music, the Lafayette Quartet is performing Murray Schafer's First Quartet. A few minutes into the piece, older members of the audience start shifting in their seats, rustling programs and exchanging whispers, while the students in the back rows sit in fascinated silence. The music has begun with a sudden fortissimo tone-cluster, with all four instruments gathered in mid-register in an aural knot. Occasionally a few quick notes dart out from one or more of the instruments, as if a skein of the knot has been yanked. Then the ball of tones reassembles in a blur and inches up and down by quarter-tone increments. "The first part of the quartet," the composer wrote in his introductory note to the score, "should give the impression of players locked together, with each trying unsuccessfully to break away from the others." The sheen of sound is not at all unpleasant, a rough but colorful knit, but it is disorienting. It seems to lack the struts which give most music a shape: there is as yet no melody, no predictable rhythm, and no key.

When he began writing string quartets, Schafer was immersed, along with colleagues at Simon Fraser University in Vancouver, in a ten-year investigation of the natural and artificial sounds that surround us in modern life. In 1976 the composer summarized this work, which he called the World

Soundscape Project, in *The Tuning of the World*, one of the most remarkable of all books about music.[97] In it Schafer describes the "sound congestion" created by the roar of traffic, the one-tone hum of electric machinery, and the other noises, at once continuous and cacophonous, that crowd our aural background. This modern soundscape contrasts with the prevailing near-silence of pre-industrial society. Throughout most of the human past, for most people, sound — a shout, an animal's call, a churchbell, footsteps, the meeting of hoe and soil — intruded upon quiet. Sounds were the foreground; the background was silence. Similarly, in most pre-urban visual landscapes, Schafer suggests, villages, church steeples, approaching figures, and distant hills stood out against simple, open backgrounds. Background and foreground were fundamental to painting because they were fundamental to the natural world that people saw. In the same way, the traditional structures of music emerged from the foreground and background of the natural soundscape, in the midst of which humans evolved.

Art mirrors life, and it organizes sensory materials to create images in its mirror. Painting imposes order on colors and shapes; drama, on human actions; music, on sounds. In the natural soundscape, the dominant characteristic is contrast: between sound and silence, and, among sounds, between long and short, loud and soft, high and low. Thus traditional musics, including European classical music, were ordered according to contrast — between loud and soft, quick and slow, theme and variation, dissonance and consonance, emotional tension and release, harmonic departure and return. One reason that music compelled people to listen was that it made sense of the natural sonic world.

Today, in industrialized countries, few people live in either the landscape or the soundscape of nature. Urban landscapes are built of straight lines, crowded forms, and gray shades. Urban soundscapes consist of a ceaseless ground bass, a shifting clamor in the streets, and, indoors, a media clatter overlaid upon the linear hum of appliances. Industrial society has flattened the contrasts among which our sense of hearing evolved, and which were the basis of musical forms. In urban life, the background has merged with the foreground. Nothing is salient in the aural landscape; there is only noise. The countryside, too, has been despoiled with sonic trash. Schafer laments that even the austere silences of the Canadian arctic, which he identifies as the root of his country's national myth, have been rent by the snowmobile and the airplane. In the modern soundscape, therefore, traditional musics are at a loss. Their time-honored natural materials have sunk into an inescapable, ubiquitous muck. The contrasts and subtleties of melody, rhythm, harmony, and dynamic variation no longer describe our aural reality.

In this sense, modernist music — especially atonal music — fulfills the responsibility of art to construct itself from the materials of our sensory life. When music does without melody and harmony, and, in the case of aleatory (chance-based) music, without a predictable rhythm, it describes the world that we now hear. So, too, does an abstract painting, without discernible figure or recognizable composition, mirror the world we now see. If the emotion communicated by such destablized music and visual art is very often anxiety, that, too, is faithful to our experience of what surrounds us. As Schafer notes, the machine-like repetitiveness of much pop music, too — and its percussive aggression, its incessant loudness, its radical simplification of melody and harmony — are accurate reflections of the urban soundscape.

When noise envelops us, noise becomes the raw material of music. The circle completes itself when music joins traffic and machinery as background static. Just as noise has produced music, music has become another noise. Sitting in their vehicles, modern listeners immerse themselves in noise-music and turn up the bass to match pitches with the roar of freeways. If *The Tuning of the World* had been published after the advent of rap, Schafer might well have described it as the music of urban violence. In rap, melody and harmony have been abandoned, and song imitates machine-gun fire and beatings. In the light of the modern soundscape, then, it only makes sense that Western music has become a troubled art, with listeners alienated from composers and every tradition in disarray. Never before, in its task of arranging the disorder of our sense impressions into patterns that are ordered and beautiful, has an art been handed raw materials of such unalloyed ugliness.

Schafer's String Quartet No. 1 is a portrait of our dilemma as captives of the modern soundscape. In the quartet, after several minutes of struggle to escape from the knot of the opening tone-cluster, the four string voices finally break free. The two violins exchange a melody that tumbles over chromatic steps with the sound of sobs. At last, figures are standing out against the background, as individuals distinct from the mass — and they are weeping. Soon all four voices make an attempt to sing together, in obedience to the cooperative paradigm of the string quartet, but they have forgotten how to blend. Twice the second violin and viola, trying out a melody together, fall out of sync — imitating, as Schafer hints in *The Tuning of the World*, the irregular clatter of belt machinery.[98] All that they know of harmonized sound is what they have heard on the assembly line. Eventually the four voices do merge, in unison or at the octave, but their collaboration disintegrates. Each breaks away in turn into a partly improvised cadenza which Schafer notates in the score by a scribble. He instructs the performers: "The impression must be one of growing frenzy — in the end almost chaos." It is the fearful fate of human voices overwhelmed by mass noise.

The last section of the quartet consists of brief quotations from earlier sections of the piece. Most are concluded by the cellist snapping a string loudly against the fingerboard. In his notes to the score, the composer calls these quotations "snapshots" — although the cello snap is omitted from the last few quotes, as if, the composer remarks, the camera has run out of film. The listeners in the audience might be archaeologists sifting among the records of a civilization that has committed suicide by deafening itself.

The noise of the industrial revolution is of course nothing new. One reason that the string quartet developed from the outdoor serenade is that it had become necessary to move the serenade indoors. In Schafer's words: "The string quartet and urban pandemonium are contemporaneous." Already in Beethoven's time, nostalgia for the soundscape of rural life had become a hallmark of European music. Beethoven's Sixth Symphony ("Pastoral") imitates a babbling brook and a peasant dance that he himself had to visit the countryside to hear. Nowadays, the village he described is engulfed by Vienna, and the brook is preserved in a city park, saved by a symphony.

In this, as so many in other ways, the musical life of our time begins with Beethoven. All pre-modernist music now serves as a pastoral. Melody and harmony are, above all, remembrances of the natural world. Audiences can be confident that a performance of music written before 1900 will recreate a record of the rural soundscape as it was perceived by a musician who still lived within reach of it. The preference of older listeners for older music, then, does not really arise from aesthetic conservatism, but from an exhaustion with urban noise. The young, still excited by the city, are ready to relish dissonance. Most listeners who are over 35 go to a concert for the same reason that they take a walk in what is left of the quiet countryside: to escape anxiety and dislocation by returning to a surrounding that is consonant with their biological memory. Thus arose the difference among the generations in Victoria as they reacted to the Lafayette's performance of the Schafer quartet. In their own ways, both the delighted students and their uncomfortable elders were responding to the music accurately. The students recognized the music as the truth; their elders heard it as all too real.

Exasperation with the clamor of modern life has led to the revival in performance of Renaissance and medieval music and to the advent of neo-medievalism, neo-romanticism, minimalism, and world music as new compositional styles. Listeners first, then composers, and finally performers have now all understood that, along with music that mirrors our modern surroundings, there must also be music that revitalizes our cultural and biological roots. Schafer, for example, left Vancouver and the shelter of the academy, retreated to a farm in Northern Ontario, and turned to opera and outdoor musical theater, using Native American and environmental themes. His String Quartet No. 2 ("Waves," 1976) imitates, as the title indicates, the sounds and motions of water. As for myself, I believe that the work of music will more and more become the work of conservation. Just as the environmental movement arose in the nineteenth century to protect unique places and now must struggle to protect the earth itself, so music, and all the arts, must now be the preservator of our natural sensory world and thus a guarantor of our sanity.

Notes

1. The Juilliard first performed for the Candlelight Concerts in 1958, the year Isidore Cohen joined the ensemble. The Juilliard entered its fiftieth year in 1996, the Candlelight series its fiftieth in 1997. With Robert Mann's retirement in 1997, none of the Juilliard's original members remains in the quartet.

2. Listen, for example, to R. Murray Schafer's fourth quartet (1989). (There is a recording by the Orford Quartet, with soprano Rosemary Landry, on Centrediscs). Settings of string quartet with soprano voice are rare, probably because of the lack of contrast. Schoenberg used soprano in his second quartet (1907-8) and Ginastera in his third (1973).

3. Twenty-seven quartets were listed in the 1965 Musical America International Directory of the Performing Arts, according to "The Boom is Real," *Chamber Music Magazine,* Spring, 1984. The more recent figures come from David Bury and Stephen Proctor, *Chamber Music in America: Status of the National Chamber Music Field: A Working Paper.* New York: Chamber Music America, 1992, p. 4-6.

4. By 1992, nearly half the school districts in the United States had made reductions in their music and other arts programs, according to a survey from that year made by the National Association of Elementary School Principals. See also Gary O. Larson, *American Canvas: An Arts Legacy for Our Communities.* Washington, D.C.: National Endowment for the Arts, 1997, p. 91ff.

5. See The Wolf Organization, "The Financial Condition of Sym-

phony Orchestras." American Symphony Orchestra League, 1992.

6. In the opinion of Dean Stein, Executive Director of Chamber Music America, the leading professional association of chamber music performers and presenters. David M. Rubin, "IsThere Life after Government Funding?" *Chamber Music*, August, 1996, p. 22. See also Rubin, "The Sun Will Come Out Tomorrow — Or Will It?" *Chamber Music*, December, 1997, p. 18.

7. RCA LM/LSC-2626, 1962.

8. *Henry V,* I, ii, 179ff.

9. There are numerous accounts of the murky origins of the quartet. I found most useful Sheila M. Nelson, *The Violin and Viola*, New York: W. W. Norton, 1972, pp. 110-115, and Paul Griffiths, *The String Quartet: A History,* New York: Thames and Hudson, 1983, pp. 9-12.

10. The composer and pedagogue Johann Joachim Quantz (1697-1773) lamented in 1752: "The viola is commonly regarded as of little importance in the musical establishment. The reason may well be that it is often played by persons who are either still beginners in the ensemble or have no particular gifts with which to distinguish themselves on the violin, or that the instrument yields all to few advantages to its players, so that able people are not easily persuaded to take it up." Quoted in Nelson, op. cit., p. 76.

11. Mozart, in particular, championed the viola, featuring it in four of his greatest works: the Sinfonia Concertante in E flat, K364 (1779), which is a double-concerto for viola and violin; the Trio in E flat, K498 (1786) for clarinet, viola, and piano; and the string quintets No. 3 in C. K515 (1787) and No. 4 in G minor, K516 (1787) for two violins, two violas, and cello.

12. For the preceding discussion of Haydn's and Mozart's early quartets, I am indebted to Griffiths, op. cit., pp. 28ff.

13. The Amateur Chamber Music Players, a service and funding organization based in New York, had a membership of

4,200 in 1996, including 700 Europeans. Lucy Miller, "From All Walks, Amateurs in America." *Chamber Music,* December, 1996, p. 20.

14. Quoted in H.C. Robbins-Landon, *Beethoven: A Documentary Study,* London: Macmillan, 1975, p. 61.

15. The late quartets are sometimes counted as six, rather than five. The composer wrote a replacement for the last movement of his Quartet No. 13, Opus 130, in B-flat major, and published the original movement, the *Grosse Fuge,* separately as Opus 133. If the *Grosse Fuge* ("Great Fugue") is counted separately, there are six late quartets, thus seventeen in all.

16. Stephen Adams, *R. Murray Schafer.* Toronto: University of Toronto Press, 1983, p. 36.

17. Andrew Dawes, "R. Murray Schafer: A Conversation with the Composer," *Strings,* May-June 1991, p. 53.

18. In conversation with the author, February 10, 1994.

19. In conversation with the author, January 23, 1994. Examples of Riley's quartets recorded by the Kronos Quartet are "Cadenza on the Night Plain," et. al, Gramavision R42J-79444, and "Salome Dances for Peace, for String Quartet (1989)," Elektra/Nonesuch 79217-4. Riley has also written for Kronos a concerto for string quartet and orchestra and a work for string quartet tuned in just intonation.

20. In conversation with the author, February 19, 1994.

21. This work, too, was written for the Kronos Quartet, and recorded by them for Elektra/Asylum/Nonesuch, 79176-2.

22. Mark Hertsgaard, *A Day in the Life: The Music and Artistry of the Beatles.* New York: Delacorte Press, 1995, pp. 132, 182.

23. For the listener interested in exploring the string quartet repertoire outlined in the foregoing pages, a Listener's Guide is included in this book as Appendix A.

24. *Kismet* was premiered in 1953 by the Los Angeles and San

Francisco Light Opera Association. The film version was released in 1955.

24a. The Lafayette plays a quartet of Amati instruments on loan from the University of Saskatchewan. Joanna's 1607 viola, built by Antonio and Hieronymus Amati, is the oldest of the instuments. Sharon's violin, by the same makers, dates from 1627; Ann's violin was made by Nicolo Amati III in 1637. Pam's cello, built by Heironymus Amati II, dates from 1690. The quartet was collected by an Icelandic-Canadian farmer, Stephen Kolbinson, and donated by him to the University of Saskatchewan in 1958.

25. For example, in the third movement of Shostakovich's Quartet No. 3, the two violins and cello pluck the strings to accompany the viola solo. For the violist's solo in the third movement of Brahms' String Quartet Opus 67, the composer directs the other players to use mutes.

26. I owe this one to Paul Yarbrough, violist of the Alexander Quartet.

27. Some early forms of vocal polyphony in Europe kept the melody in a lower voice — thus the term "tenor," or holder — while one or more voices above it sang a descant for ornamentation. This form exploited the greater power of the full male voice in comparison with the higher falsetto or the boy's treble. If medieval choirs had consisted of mixed voices — men and women together — the power of the soprano voice would perhaps have made descants much less attractive. The use of the tenor voice as the melody-holder survives in all-male barbershop singing, in which the top line is devoted to accompaniment and is sung falsetto. In the history of string quartets, Schubert was the composer fondest of descants, which he assigned to the first violin above a second violin melody.

28. Strictly speaking, both Hindustani and Karnatak musics — the musics of Northern and Southern India — are performed not in keys but in ragas, which are complex scales, often amounting to simple tunes. The soloist elaborates the raga to

create improvised melodies. The drone instrument — often the tambura, a four-stringed lute — meanwhile repeats the home note of the raga. A similar effect might be created by repeating middle C throughout a complex improvisation of a simple C-major tune. See Bonnie C. Wade, *Music in India: The Classical Traditions.* Englewood Cliffs, NJ: Prentice Hall, 1979.

29. Nelson, op. cit., p. 1-6.

30. Elliot Forbes, ed., *Thayer's Life of Beethoven.* Princeton, NJ: Princeton University Press, 1967, p. 261.

31. Ibid., p. 976-77.

32. On another visit to Germany, in 1877, Borodin made a detour to Heidelberg to retrace the steps of their courtship. He stayed at the same inn — "the old room, the old staircase," he wrote home to Protopopova, "and when left to myself I could not help crying like a child." Quoted in Alfred Habets, *Borodin and Liszt,* tr. Rosa Newmarch. London: Digby, Long, and Co., 1895, reprinted by AMS Press, New York, 1977, p. 95.

33. Serge Dianin, *Borodin,* tr. Robert Lord. London: Oxford University Press, 1963, p. 246. Dianin's father was one of Borodin's favorite students and his mother one of the childless Borodins' adopted daughters.

34. The classical formalism that Joanna alludes to is evident throughout the piece. All four movements, for example, are in sonata form. Also, the movements are tied to each other by several musical constants, among them a sustained A that appears in numerous contexts, and the rising or falling fourths common to several of the melodies.

35. Letter to Marc-André Souchay, October 15, 1842, quoted in Andrew Storr, *Music and the Mind.* New York: Free Press, p. 65.

36. The Lafayette has recorded Borodin's Quartet No. 2 for Dorian Recordings, DOR-90203, 1995. Shostakovich's Quartet No. 3 and Stravinsky's Three Pieces for String Quartet are also on the disk.

37. For example, J. Keith Murnigham and Donald E. Conlon, "The Dynamics of Work Groups: A Study of British String Quartets." *Administrative Science Quarterly*, 36 (1991): 165-186, and Tory Butterworth, "The Detroit String Quartet", in J. Richard Hackman, ed. *Groups That Work (and Those That Don't): Creating Conditions for Effective Teamwork*. San Francisco: Jossey-Bass, 1990. pp. 207-24.

38. It is not uncommon for quartets, both amateur and professional, to be formed by siblings. Two members of the Busch Quartet were brothers, as were two members of the Budapest Quartet. Young contemporary quartets continue the trend: in the Cuarteto Latinoamericano, a Mexican ensemble, all the players except the violist are brothers, while the Ying Quartet, an American ensemble, consists of three brothers and their sister.

39. Colin Hampton, in conversation with the author, December 17, 1993; also Tully Potter, "Farewell to Academia." *The Strad*, January, 1986, pp. 680-688.

40. Nat Brandt, *Con Brio: Four Russians Called the Budapest String Quartet*. New York: Oxford University Press, 1993, p. 126 ff.

41. Edith Eisler, "The Guarneri Quartet: On Rehearsing, Playing without a First Violinist, and Staying Together." *Strings*, July-August 1992, p. 37.

42. In conversation with the author, not for attribution.

43. Colin Hampton, cellist of the Griller Quartet, recalls this anecdote concerning a late nineteenth-century German quartet: when on tour, in the morning in their hotel, the other members of the quartet waited for the first violinist to appear before they dared sit down to breakfast.

44. For example, in Britain, Irvine Arditti of the Arditti Quartet and Levon Chilingirian of the Chilingirian Quartet; in the Czech Republic, Jiri Panocha of the Panocha Quartet.

45. In conversation with the author, April 18, 1994. Quoted in part in David Rounds, "Quartet Tradition, Russian-style." *The Strad*, June, 1995, p. 582ff.

46. Brandt, op. cit., pp. 35, 52.

47. "Perfect Discord." *The Sunday Times Magazine,* November 16, 1980. Quoted in Suzanne Rosza-Lovett,*The Amadeus: Forty Years in Pictures and Words.* London: privately published, 1988, p. 74.

48. ibid.

49. I observed Dubinsky lead a rehearsal of his piano trio, The Borodin Trio, and also a rehearsal of Tchaikovsky's string sextet, "Souvenir de Florence," in Vancouver in April, 1994.

50. In conversation with the author, not for attribution.

51. Murnigham, op. cit., p. 175.

52. Ibid., p. 183.

53. Barbara Sand, "Quartet of Decades." *The Strad,* October, 1986, p. 395.

54. Rounds, op cit., p. 585.

55. David Blum, *The Art of Quartet Playing: The Guarerni Quartet in Conversation with David Blum.* Ithaca, NY: Cornell University Press, 1986, p. 54.

56. Despite its determination, as I have mentioned, to maintain individuality in its voices, the Juilliard does not make this balance error.

57. In answer to a question by the author during a pre-concert lecture, San Francisco, January 18, 1994.

58. The Mill Valley (California) Chamber Music Society, in its announcement of its 1993-94 season.

59. By exception, Robert Mann, who was the first violinist of the Juilliard Quartet for fifty years and who was, until his retirement in 1997, the most eminent quartet player in North America, is known by name to many quartet audiences. But few could name the violist of the Juilliard, Samuel Rhodes, although he played with Mann for almost thirty years.

Alexander Schneider, second violinist of the Budapest Quartet, became famous — but only after he left the quartet for ten years to pursue an independent career.

60. In conversation with the author, February 11, 1994.

61. David Bury and Stephen Proctor, *Chamber Music in America: Status of the National Chamber Music Field: A Working Paper.* New York: Chamber Music America, 1992, p. 11. Forty percent was the amount before management commissions; after commissions, the cost of travel was closer to fifty percent of performance earnings.

62. Ibid., p. 5, 11.

63. David M. Rubin, "Six Quartets in Search of an Auditor: The Economic Side of Ensemble Life." *Chamber Music*, Fall 1989, p. 16 ff.

64. A survey conducted for Chamber Music America in 1987 found that, on a sample of chamber music programs in the United States, five percent of the compositions were written during the Baroque period, thirty-nine percent during the Classical Period (almost entirely Haydn, Mozart, Beethoven, and Schubert), seventeen percent from the Romantic period (from Mendelssohn to Dvořák), and thirty-nine percent from the twentieth century. Of the ten most performed composers, only Bartók, Shostakovich, and Ravel wrote music after the First World War. David M. Rubin, "Beyond the Chamber Music Hit Parade, Part 1." *Chamber Music*, Fall 1987, p. 10. Fifty-five percent of respondents to a different survey sent by the San Antonio Chamber Music Society to its subscribers in 1992 said they wanted to hear contemporary music "rarely", while another seventeen percent wrote in "NEVER." Diane Cumming Persellin and Robert H. Persellin, "Mired in the Nineteenth Century: Music Preferences of a Chamber Music Audience." *American String Teacher*, Summer 1993, p. 40.

65. Katherine L. Hurley, "Canadian Quartet Heritage." *The Strad*, November, 1993, p. 1089. The history of the Pro Arte Quartet

was recorded by Martha Blum in *The Pro Arte Quartet: 50 Years.* University of Wisconsin School of Music, 1991.

66. The Orford disbanded in 1991.

67. The history of the Candlelight Concerts to 1966 is recorded in Stowell Rounds, *The First Twenty Years: 1947-1967,* reissued by the Wilton (Connecticut) Library Association, 1967.

68. See n. 3.

69. Hurley, op. cit., p. 1091.

70. Bury and Proctor, op. cit., p. 6.

71. Ibid.

72. Op. cit., p. 13.

73. Op cit., p. 5. According to Chamber Music America, most of the organizations that present chamber music concerts in the United States belong to one of three types. About a fifth of all presenting organizations are professionally managed, independent non-profit corporations, which stage chamber concerts, along with solo recitals, jazz concerts, and dance, in the larger cities. Another fifth are small organizations known as volunteer presenters — although many employ a part-time paid director in addition to volunteers. These groups, located in suburbs, city neighborhoods, and provincial towns, present only chamber music and recitals, usually in churches. Another third of the chamber music presenters are colleges and universities, which sponsor a medley of performances, classical and popular, in on-campus halls, as a service to their faculty, students, and neighbors. Another sixth of the presenters are summer festivals, and the last tenth includes museums, independent halls (such as Carnegie Hall in New York), arts councils of local governments, and self-presenting musical organizations such as symphony orchestra associations that stage chamber music series.

74. According to Chamber Music America's *1996 Membership*

Directory, which lists 89 string quartets, and Hurley, op. cit., p. 1091.

75. "Twenty-nine percent of the responding presenters are located in the Northeast, 24% in the North Central region, 20% in the South, and 22% in the West." Bury and Proctor, op. cit., p. 17.

76. Private support for the arts in the United States totaled $10.23 billion in 1992 and just under $10 billion in 1995, according to *Giving USA: The Annual Report on Philanthropy for the Year 1995*, New York: AAFRC Trust for Philanthropy, 1996, p. 25. Quoted in Larson, *American Canvas*, op. cit., p. 50. By contrast, local government support for the 50 largest local arts agencies increased by 35.3% from 1990 to 1996; these 50 agencies (among nearly 4,000 in the country) accounted for 32% of all funding. Larson, op. cit., p. 85.

77. The number of annual attendances per concertgoer in 1992 was 2.6, for a total of 60.3 million attendances. *Arts Participation in America: 1982-1992*, Research Division Report #27. Washington, DC: National Endowment for the Arts, October, 1993, p. 2-3.

78. Richard A. Peterson, et. al., "Age and Arts Participation, with a Focus on the Baby Boom Cohort." Research Division Report #34. Washington, DC.: National Endowment for the Arts, 1996, p. 2.

79. Bury and Proctor, op. cit., p. 24.

80. See David Rounds, "Lighting a Candle for Music," *The Strad*, September, 1995, p. 908-13.

81. In conversation with the author, February 3, 1994.

82. In conversation with the author, December 28, 1993.

83. In conversation with the author, February 3, 1994.

84. The dates given in this section are years of composition, as listed in Michael Kennedy, *The Oxford Dictionary of Music*. New York: Oxford University Press, 1985. Life spans dates

are also from this source. The composers are listed within their groups in chronological order according to their dates of birth.

85. The count varies. There are sixty-eight if the Seven Last Words, Op. 50-56, are considered (as they are usually performed) as one work; if the unfinished Opus 103 is included; and if only the four genuine quartets of Opus 2 are counted. See Griffiths, op. cit., pp. 11-12.

86. Maynard Solomon doubts the truth of this tradition. *Mozart*, New York: Harper Collins, 1995, p. 442.

87. The reach of these E flat chords is indicated by this remark by David Harrington, the first violinist and leader of the Kronos Quartet: "The opening chords of the Opus 127 reverberate through everything I do." Yet Kronos rarely performs music written before 1970. (In conversation with the author, May 26 1993.)

88. Shostakovich, who was Mendelssohn's equal as a technician, wrote two one-movement string octets: Prelude, Opus 11a, and Scherzo, Opus 11b (1924-25)

89. Centrediscs 3990, 4090, 1990.

90. In conversation with the author, January 23, 1994.

91. Solomon Volkov, ed., *Testimony: The Memoirs of Dmitri Shostakovich*. Tr. Antonia W. Bouis. New York: Harper and Row, 1979.

92. See Ian MacDonald, *The New Shostakovich*. Boston: Northeastern University Press, 1990, and Rostislav Dubinsky, *Stormy Applause: Making Music in a Workers' State*. New York: Hill and Wang, 1989.

93. MacDonald, op. cit., p. 132-3.

94. Dubinsky, op. cit., p. 278ff.

95. Volkov, op. cit., p. 155.

96. MacDonald, op. cit., p. 181-83.

97. R. Murray Schafer, *The Tuning of the World*. Toronto: McClellan and Stewart, 1977.

98. Ibid., p. 113, as noted by Stephen Adams, op. cit., p. 125.